PROPHETIC WORLDS

To Bruce Hamilton
with best wishes

Christopher L Miller

"when christendom shall have passed into Oregon and other heathen and dark regions, her best population, carrying with them the ever-burning lights of the gospel; then will mankind realize something like the halcyon era of universal peace."

HALL JACKSON KELLEY

"Soon there will come from the rising sun a different kind of man from any you have yet seen, who will bring with them a book and will teach you everything, and after that the world will fall to pieces."

THE SPOKAN PROPHET

Prophetic Worlds

Indians and Whites
on the Columbia Plateau

Christopher L. Miller

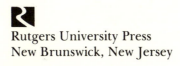
Rutgers University Press
New Brunswick, New Jersey

Library of Congress Cataloging in Publication Data
Miller, Christopher L., 1950–
  Prophetic worlds

  Bibliography:p.
  Includes index.
    1.Indians of North America—Columbia River Valley—
Missions.   2. Indians of North America—Columbia River
Valley—Religion and mythology.   3. Columbia River
Valley—Church history.   I. Title.
E78.C64M55   1985   299'.7997   84-18013
ISBN 0-8135-1084-8

FOR ELLEN, as an eternal monument
in loving memory of her father and
my friend, Chilton O'Brien

Contents

Acknowledgments

As with all books (especially an author's first), this project would have been impossible without a great deal of assistance from a large number of people. First, I must credit the faculty and staff of the University of California, Santa Barbara for initiating me into the mysteries of the historical profession. I am especially indebted to Roderick Nash, Richard E. Oglesby, J. Sears McGee, and Robert Kelley. Special note must be made of my friend and mentor Wilbur R. Jacobs, who has provided both wise criticism and steadfast support.

I must also thank the faculty and staff of Lewis and Clark College, who provided me with an institutional affiliation and assistance while I was conducting the research for this study. Of special assistance were the acting president, John E. Brown, and the staff of the Aubrey Watzek Library. I am particularly indebted to Vicki Kreimeyer, who often worked miracles to get me rare books and other odd materials. The staffs of the Portland Public Library and the Oregon Historical Society were also of enormous assistance.

I also owe a large debt to my colleagues and students at Rutgers University, who provided a valuable (if sometimes a captive) sounding board for many of the ideas that appear in this study. I cannot begin to set a value on my three-year association with Calvin Martin, who has provided constant support, criticism, fellowship, and inspiration. I have also enjoyed and profited from my association with Barbara M. Tucker, Allen Howard, James W. Reed, and John R. Gillis.

Other colleagues around the country have also provided incalculable assistance. I am particularly indebted to Angelo Anastasio, who was very generous with his time and knowledge from the inception of this project. Deward E. Walker has also provided much needed criticism and advice. I am also indebted to Anne C. Rose and Mary Young for insightful criticisms. Finally, I owe a great debt to computer genius A. P. Warnshuis, who taught me the value of electronic data and word processing and followed that up with sensitive and intelligent tutelage.

The last debts to be mentioned are the largest. First, to my parents, who, though leery of my career choice, backed me up and never failed to support my efforts. Second, to my late father-in-law, Chilton O'Brien, who provided more inspiration and support than can be expressed. I only wish that he might have lived to see the final product. Finally, to Ellen O'Brien Miller, who has been a participant in the production of this work since the very beginning. She has read every word of every version and has never failed to provide worthwhile advice and intelligent criticism. More important, she provided the emotional support that kept me afloat through the academic maelstrom. I regret that so much of the burden fell to her and hope that we may each glide on calmer waters in the future.

Introduction

This is the story of the convergence of two very different worlds. Through a process so bizarre as to seem providential, Native Americans who lived on the Columbia Plateau and Euro-Americans who lived in the United States each came to regard the other as the most significant agent in the working out of a millenarian scheme. Surface similarities between these very different nineteenth-century religious movements led the prophets of each to conclude that the other was in complete agreement and was progressing toward the same final goal. Peering through lenses tinted by true belief, neither could see that their worlds were actually on a collision course. By the time they did, proximity made evasive action impossible and the two worlds crashed together with cataclysmic results. As though in compliance with prophecy, the Indian world cracked and then fell to pieces, leaving its occupants struggling to find a place in the world that survived.[1]

It is a story very different from others that have been told concerning this meeting. Even a cursory scan of the bibliography

1

will reveal the great wealth of books and articles dealing with Protestant missionaries, Plateau Indians, and their mid-nineteenth-century relationship. Several of these are excellent and provide marvelous insights into the complex processes that threw these two groups into contact. Clifton Jackson Phillips, Robert F. Berkhofer, and even Presbyterian ex-missionary Clifford M. Drury do an excellent job of describing the missionary forces; Lucellus V. McWhorter, Alvin Josephy, and especially Deward E. Walker, Jr., provide remarkable insights into the Indian side of the story.[2] The problem is that none of these look at the converging groups under a common lens. As a result, none come to grips with the fact that both missionaries and Indians were reacting to self-perception and to their perception of each other, leading to a peculiar pattern of historical interaction.

Some readers will not agree with the idea that perceptions are significant to historical behavior because they insist that such intellectual formulations are merely window dressing for more objective real-world processes like the dialectic or evolution, that human behavior is entirely rational, and that ideas and attitudes are merely rationalizations. Indeed, historical developments may be rational over the course of what Fernand Braudel has called the *longue durée*, but it is the height of reductionism to assert that participants in historical events were aware of such processes and were consciously acting upon them.[3] No less an empirical behaviorist than Berkhofer has made this point most forcefully. In a recent address, he emphasized that one of the leding fallacies in history as it is practiced today is the assumption that historical figures understood the nature of their situation and based perfectly rational responses on a complete awareness of all of the potential implications of their actions.[4] Such flagrant disregard for the complexities of human motivation has led us to credit our ancestors with a godlike omniscience. This, in turn, has forced us to invent devious plots or to question the moral fiber of these people in order to explain why they did not act on their all-encompassing knowledge and behave as we think they should have.

I have avoided such reductionism by using the tools of ethnohistory to look behind the simple story of Indian and white contact on the Plateau. As explained by one of its more articulate spokesmen, ethnohistory involves "*the use of historical and ethnological methods and materials to gain knowledge of the nature and causes of change in a culture defined by ethnological concepts and categories.*" "Whether we consider ethnohistory a form of cultural history or a sub-discipline of cultural anthropology," he goes on, "we can agree that it represents a union of history and ethnology, whose purpose is to produce scholarly offspring who bear the diachronic dimensions of history and the synchronic sensitivity of ethnology."[5]

To produce this offspring, ethnohistorians must draw upon a wide variety of sources, including "maps, music, paintings, pictographs, folklore, oral tradition, ecology, site exploration, archaeological artifacts (especially trade goods), museum collections, enduring customs, language, and place names, as well as a richer variety of written sources."[6] Thus, to the ethnohistorian, the mélange of myths, folk stories, theological speculations, and social and religious behavior revealed in these sources make them the equivalent of the written literature upon which white histories are based. Myths and folk stories can no longer be passed off as quaint stories dreamed up by the childlike imaginations of "primitives." Calvin Martin has stated this most forcefully in his prize-winning book *Keepers of the Game*:

> For many readers the story which follows will seem a fantasy because it is suffused with native oral literature and, especially, spiritual beliefs. However fantastic, this core of belief is the absolutely crucial context of the Indian's familiar environment—the realm in which he operated. He took his behavioral environment completely seriously and conducted himself, even when in the presence of skeptical whites, according to its principles. . . . To neglect this "fantasy," then, would be to risk inappropriately fantastic, because Westernized, interpretations of baffling events in this early period of contact history.[7]

By probing these oral traditions carefully and critically, it is possible to construct a history of the Indians' intellectual world.

Of course the process is not easy. After all, the Indian idea system is foreign to us, suffused as it is with tales of miraculous happenings, spirit-induced illnesses, and rather unusual concepts of time, cause, and effect. Yet, a perusal of Keith Thomas's study of folk beliefs in England reveals that our seventeenth-century ancestors had ideas no less foreign to current ways of thinking, a fact that has not deterred us from pursuing intellectual histories of early modern Europe.[8] Thus the ideas and attitudes of the Indian participants in Indian-white contacts are available to us and must be considered alongside those of the white participants if we are to gain an accurate understanding of what transpired.

So far, I have referred to Indians and whites as if these categories were internally consistent and mutually exclusive. This oversimplification stems from the generality of the discussion and not from a lack of awareness of the actual complexity of the situation. Though the field of ethnohistory is permeated with controversy, one fact that none deny is that no two cultures are identical.[9] Different groups obviously reacted to white contact in somewhat different ways. As Martin points out,

> It is necessary to make these clarifications lest the reader get the erroneous impression that the native societies occupying this huge swath of land were culturally and socially homogeneous. There were, indeed, many congruencies among them, especially in their abstract culture, but these must not be taken for granted. One of the more valuable lessons that ethnologists have taught historians is that they should pay closer attention to cultural boundaries separating aboriginal societies.[10]

This being the case, while Martin's study of the Indians of eastern Canada is exemplary, it certainly does not exhaust the possibilities of this ethnointellectual historical method. In fact, by yielding such a wealth of interpretive insight, Martin's work mandates the application of the method to all of the ethnic groups for which we have the necessary ethnographic data. Only thus can the patterns of Indian-white contact be demythologized and liberated from baseless assumptions concerning Indian motivation.

The Columbia Plateau is one cultural area for which we possess a great deal of ethnographic data. Ever since the pioneer days of ethnology, such masters as Franz Boas and Verne F. Ray have been drawn to this area. The works of these and other scholars form a library of ethnological information unsurpassed in volume and quality. The Plateau is uniquely suitable, therefore, for the application of this new historical methodology.

Conjoined with this opportunity is an acute necessity. Although much is known about Plateau ethnology, the history of the Plateau people has been highly mythologized. Interestingly, most treatments are overwhelmingly sympathetic. From the first white descriptions of the area and its people to the most recent historical works, the Plateau dwellers have been consistently described in superlatives: "friendly, pleasant, and inclined toward peace"; "the most intelligent Indians that I had ever seen"; "the wilderness gentry of the Pacific Northwest."[11] Furthermore, historical works ranging from James Penny Boyd's 1891 article through Robert I. Burns's and Merrill Beal's recent books have depicted the Plateau people simply as innocent victims of white perfidy.[12] Even the general who was responsible for the attack upon and eventual defeat of the Nez Perce in 1877 compared them to victims of the Spanish Inquisition.[13]

The almost storybook quality of the region's past historical treatment has misled recent efforts. The impression left by such descriptions is that these people were simply too innocent or too polite to resist encroachment by avaricious whites. Even Josephy's *The Nez Perce Indians and the Opening of the Northwest*, which is otherwise laudably sophisticated, leaves this impression.[14] As Wilbur R. Jacobs has pointed out, "If we cannot be proud of the history of Indian-white relations in . . . America, we must also recognize that this is not a simple story to tell."[15] We should, therefore, be leery of "simple" stories about "noble savages" and "grasping Anglos." As ideologically satisfying as these may be, they are probably no more accurate than simple stories about ignoble savages and altruistic civilization bearers. Unless we put aside idealized perceptions of these people and deal instead with their own ideas and perceptions, we will be left with inaccurate pictures of the historical situation.

I offer this essay as a corrective to the one-sided and idealized literature that has predominated in the treatment of Plateau history. I offer it not as an authoritative narrative nor as an exhaustive work of original research, but as a brief illustration of how the mass of materials listed in the bibliography may be interpreted. I do not wish the reader to come away with a catalog of data so much as an appreciation of the complex history of Indian-white contact on the Plateau as it was experienced and understood by the participants. I hope it will also lead the reader to apply similar corrective thinking to the broader subject of Indian-white relations at large.

CHAPTER 1

The Plateau World

The Columbia Plateau is a land of contradictions. Noted for its snow-capped peaks, much of the region is a flat grassland. In many spots the topography is identical to the greasewood deserts of the arid Southwest, yet the Columbia-Snake drainage system carries a huge volume of water through its very heartland. Much area is forbidding to plant and animal life, yet the wide variety of climates and the rich riverine resources have long provided an attractive habitat.[1] It is a land that challenges its occupants and forces them to to excel in order to survive. Like the Old Testament wilderness, it was a perfect place for a confrontation between prophets.

Like the area itself, Plateau cultures seem filled with contradictions. The descriptions of Plateau life recorded by the first Euro-Americans to enter the area made the culture sound like an odd mixture of Plains and Northwest Coast lifestyles. This led early analysts to conclude that there was no Plateau culture per se and that the area was merely a fuzzy frontier between two fully articulated culture areas. This impression lasted until 1933,

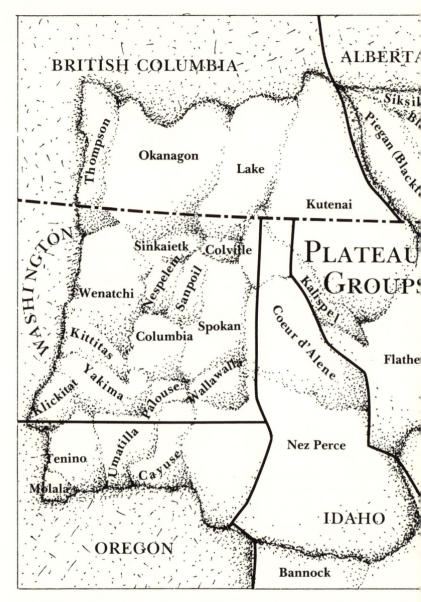

▲ Approximate locations of Indian groups mentioned in the text (circa 173

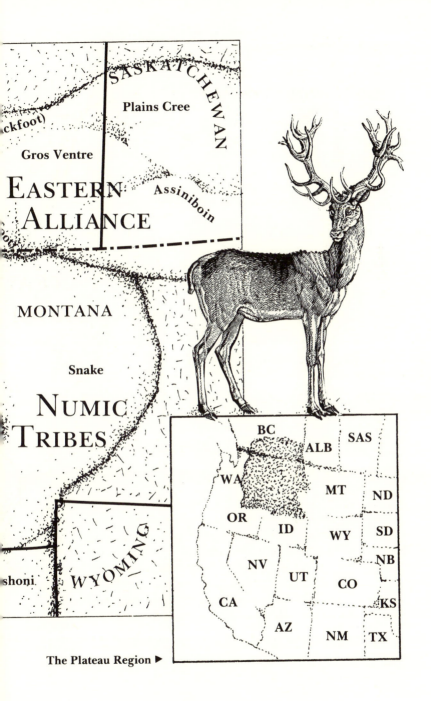

SASKATCHEWAN

Plains Cree

ckfoot)

Gros Ventre

Assiniboin

EASTERN
ALLIANCE

MONTANA

Snake

NUMIC
TRIBES

shoni

WYOMING

BC

ALB   SAS

WA

MT   ND

OR   ID

WY   SD

NV   UT   NB

CA   CO   KS

AZ

NM   TX

The Plateau Region ▶

when Ray's groundbreaking ethnological research finally demonstrated that the Plateau was a culture area in its own right.[2] From that point it became possible to retrace both the history and culture of the Plateau people.

It now appears that the Plateau people have been adapting to this rigorous territory for at least 14,500 years. For millennia, the people in the greater Pacific Northwest shared what has been called the "Northern Forest culture." Consisting of an amorphous blend of coastal, subarctic, and desert characteristics, this culture exploited the wide variety of riverine and other resources in an efficient but adaptive fashion. During these millennia, various groups became more specifically adapted to their own environmental niches, and eventually the Northern Forest culture split into Coastal, Plateau, and Desert elements. Because of the long duration of the process and the continued close contact between the resulting cultures, it is difficult to pinpoint the exact moment when this division was completed, but archaeologists have concluded that the terminal date was about A.D. 1300.[3]

The Plateau world that emerged was divided into two distinct linguistic sections. In the northern area the predominant language was based on a proto-Salish ancestral tongue and was broken into at least fifteen related languages including Spokan, Coeur d'Alene, and Flathead. The southern section was occupied by the descendants of Penutian speakers who had divided into three distinct language families.[4]

Though it has been determined that these two major language groupings formed quite separate "communities" or "congregations," the weight of anthropological and ethnological evidence indicates that linguistic boundaries had little significance in terms of culture. That some Penutian-speaking peoples had much more in common with their Salish neighbors than with their colinguists and vice versa indicates that, while people varied a great deal on the Plateau, they formed a single ethnological entity nonetheless.[5]

To get around the problem of how to isolate and describe this entity, Ray analyzed the Sanpoil, a small isolated, Salish-speaking group, so that he could generalize from them to the aboriginal culture of the area.[6] His research indicates that during aboriginal times the people on the Plateau were organized around shared political principles. The basic unit was the village, each village with its own headman, who was subject to no outside authorities. All matters of government were decided by the headman, his subchief, and all the inhabitants of the village. Though chieftainship most often passed from father to son, the people named the headman and had the power to alter the order of succession or to remove a headman who no longer met their needs. Decisions were by acclamation, and occupants who disagreed simply moved to another village.[7]

It is impossible to know to what degree individual villages coalesced into tribelike structures. It would appear that there was no large-scale political integration and that the only intergroup bonds were linguistic and familial. Even the latter may be somewhat overstated. Resettlement and cooperation between villages associated with different "tribes" appear to have been as frequent as between those within the same "tribe." Thus, while some degree of linguistic or ethnic preference divided the Plateau among various "tribes," the village was probably the only constant organizational unit in aboriginal times.[8]

This scheme of political organization seems loose and highly parochial in its scope, but it was only part of a much larger, albeit fluid, organizational structure. Larger units formed and disbanded depending on need. Tasks calling for intensive cooperative labor demanded larger organizations, which formed regardless of ethnic or linguistic affiliations.[9] These temporary larger units were defined by the network of relationships woven by the migrations of individuals and families from village to village and "tribe" to "tribe."[10]

Though the larger organizations were only temporary, the pattern of forming them was permanent, and only those groups that participated in shared tasks can be described as aboriginal Plateau tribes. These, according to Angelo Anastasio, were the Cayuse, Umatilla, Wayam, Wasco, Wishram, Klickitat, Yakima, Wallawalla, Nez Perce, Palouse, Kittitas, Columbia, Flathead,

Coeur d'Alene, Wenatchi, Chelan, Spokan, Sanpoil, Methow, Nespelem, Kalispel, Sinkaietk, and Colville. Some groups, like the Klamath, Kutenai, Okanagon, and many others, also participated in tasks but were not part of the permanent cooperative pattern.[11]

Aboriginal tasks and the accompanying schemes of organization revolved around the changing of the seasons and the availability of staple food sources. Fishing, hunting, and food gathering—the basic components of the Plateau economy—each had its own season and location. This forced the Indians of the Plateau to follow a widely varied round of activities and to lead a semisedentary life in which they often engaged and disengaged themselves from cooperative task groups.[12]

The cycle began in the spring with the reappearance of migrating birds and hibernating mammals. As the days lengthened, the Plateau people abandoned the underground houses they had wintered in and built temporary mat lodges aboveground. The men began hunting for waterfowl and rabbits and gathering river mussels while the women combed the river banks for early edible roots. As the weather improved, the people dismantled the winter houses and began their migration to the spring root-digging grounds. Task groups of four or five families formed and split off from the main group, each going to its own favorite digging spots. The winter village was completely abandoned except for the old and infirm, who remained with a few able-bodied caretakers to guard the village site and the cached equipment that would be needed when the village reformed in the fall.

At the digging grounds, the mat lodges were rebuilt. The women spent their days gathering roots, including bitterroot, wild carrots, wild onions, and wapato. The camps moved often in order to be near fresh fields. If camp was near a productive stream, the men would fish for trout or sturgeon, and if game was nearby, they might hunt for rabbits or antelope.[13] Toward the end of May, fishing began to take precedence over bulb digging as the spring run of salmon began to work its way up the rivers and streams. Summer base camps were then set up at favorite fishing sites. Often gigantic multilingual task villages were formed at popular locations.

In summer, the men became the most significant economic contributors, fishing or hunting depending on the fish runs and the availability of game. They speared, hooked, netted, or trapped silver and chinook salmon; steelhead, cutthroat, and lake trout; lamprey eels; suckers; and sturgeon with efficiency reflecting thousands of years of practice and increasing technological sophistication. The women cooked and dried the fish and stored them for winter use. The women also spent time gathering serviceberries, chokecherries, huckle-berries, strawberries, currants, and other wild fruits, some for immediate consumption, others to dry and store. Seeds, including sunflower seeds and some grass seeds, they gathered and stored for later use as well.[14]

As fall approached, the summer villages prepared to break up. Beginning about the first of September, some task groups split off, moving to the upland prairies to gather camas bulbs or to dig kouse roots in the dry soil on the higher slopes. Meanwhile, other task groups remained at the fishing grounds to take advantage of the fall salmon run and to hunt local game and harvest vegetable foods. The men engaged in intensive hunting, shooting deer, elk, black bear, grizzly bear, mountain sheep, or whatever other game was available. Birds, including prairie chickens, blue grouse, geese, and ducks were taken in great numbers. Beaver and otter, considered great delicacies, were also shot or trapped.[15]

Most of these hunting parties stayed in the Bitterroot and other western mountain ranges, but some followed well-known foot trails to the Plains country, where they joined the Pend d'Oreille and Flathead in hunting buffalo. These groups, called *khoo-say-nee* (migrating people) by the Nez Perce, stayed out on the Plains for anywhere from six months to two years. Because they did not have the means to bring back much meat, Herbert Spinden has concluded that these men, women, and children went solely to eat their fill. They did carry back robes, horns, and other objects, however, and these became valuable commodities in intertribal trade.[16]

Beginning in about the middle of October, all the task groups except the *khoo-say-nee* started to reconvene at the winter village sites. They nearly always returned to the same village they had left the previous spring, but occasionally some who had joined a task group from another village would change their residence to stay with their new friends. In the waning days of Indian summer, the subterranean houses were rebuilt and the cached winter equipment was rescued and replaced with the dried fish, meat, and vegetables gathered over the previous nine months.

When winter closed in, the women spent their time making baskets, mats, and clothing as well as doing the basic daily tasks of cooking and watching the children. The men spent most of their time sleeping, playing games, and telling stories. Even though they had large stores of food, the men did occasional winter hunting or ice fishing.[17] Winter was also the time when children received their education. Girls watched and helped their mothers sew and cook, while boys listened to their fathers' stories about hunting or warfare. The greater part of the educational program consisted of listening to traditional folktales. Convention dictated that these stories could only be told in the winter. The children were gathered together and, while they ate treats like dried meat or *uppa* (dried root bread), the oldest people in the village told them the stories that contained the accumulated knowledge of their people. As one Nez Perce source summarized this educational process:

> By hearing these adventures again and again, the child gathered a great deal of practical information about his own physical surroundings. For example, the story, "Skunk Goes Looking for His Scent," mentions the names of twenty-two plants and tells whether they taste sweet or bitter. "Tsikh-tsikh-itsim-Boy" tells us that good arrows may be made from serviceberry twigs that are dried by the fire. Many legends name and describe various as-

pects of geography of the Nez Perce's home territory and neighboring regions.[18]

More important, the folktales were intended to help children
grow into moral people by teaching them the ethical standards
to which their behavior was expected to conform and the types
of punishments that followed the breach of these standards.[19]
The telling of these stories was not the only break in the mo-
notonous winter routine. At midwinter, when the snow had
crusted over sufficiently to allow travel, the great religious ceremonial season began. Central to this season was the winter dance
complex. These dances were so important that one Plateau ethnologist called them "their most sacred and mystical ceremony."[20] They were held to celebrate the most important religious phenomenon on the Plateau: the receipt of guardian
spirits by the members of the host group.
The guardian spirit complex was universal on the Plateau.[21]
Generally, Plateau children went on their initial spirit quest
when they were about ten years old. At that time, a child would
be sent to some especially sacred place where, all alone, he or she
would fast and wait for a vision. In this vision the child would be
visited by one of the nonhuman entities with whom the Plateau
people had social relations, and the spirit of this animal, object,
plant, or phenomenon would enter into a task relationship with
the child. Throughout his or her life, the human would refer to
this spirit as his or her "partner" or "power."[22]
Once child and spirit entered into a relationship, the spirit demanded certain types of behavior from the recipient. Generally
there were restrictions about killing or damaging the corporeal
form of the animal or object that served as the guardian spirit.[23]
The spirit might also set specific conditions that had to be maintained in order for its protection to remain in force. For example, a person might not enjoy spiritual protection if he hunted
in the rain or if his shield or club touched some proscribed object. As one Nez Perce informant expressed it, "If your power is
in feathers which you place at a certain height, and your wife

throws them down, or they fall down, then the power you had in those feathers is destroyed for all time. Your prayer has been killed. But if everything is handled right and you are true, your Waykin [guardian spirit] will surely help you when there is danger."[24]

As this example indicates, although the spirits were possessed of great powers, they were also subject to many of the same foibles that plagued human beings, particularly that of taking offense at real or imagined slights. If the spirit believed that the human partner had violated the mutually agreed upon ethical code, the guardian would withdraw its protection, breaking the line of communication between the physical and metaphysical realms. Such withdrawal left the human without direction and protection and was one of the major causes of disease in the Indian world of the Plateau. In fact, all afflictions had a spiritual significance. Most often, a person brought these on him or herself through ethical transgressions, but sometimes diseases were caused by especially powerful people manipulating physical and spiritual things through black magic.[25]

As potentially dangerous as these spirit relations were, they were essential to leading a successful life. In exchange for living up to the contract with the spirit, the recipient was endowed with mental or physical characteristics and pronounced skills in areas especially associated with the spirit's corporeal form. For example, a deer spirit could make a child a fast runner; a wolf spirit might endow its protégé with great hunting skill. The spirit also taught the child a spirit song and told him or her how to make a sacred bundle, both of which helped the child to concentrate and use his or her spiritual powers. Through this power, the man or woman gained a certain amount of protection from natural and supernatural dangers. In addition, the guardian spirit warned its human partner of impending hazards through dreams and visions.[26] In a very real sense, the spirit provided the steering mechanism that guided a person through the hazards of life, making him or her an important contributor to the groups with which he or she was associated.

That is what the winter dances celebrated. Though held by

some quite different groups, the dances were remarkably similar everywhere on the Plateau. They were hosted by people who possessed guardian spirits. Each dance would last for several days. Evenings were spent in performing spirit dances and singing the songs that the guardians had taught their human partners. This often led to singing competitions and comparative demonstrations of magical power like the *toe-ya-khin*, in which singers would try to put rivals into a trance by touching them while they sang. The balance of the time was spent in feasting, gambling, and gift giving.[27] The latter was of special importance and often flamboyantly done. It was almost universal that the members of the host group would contribute something of value to a common fund that was then distributed to the guests at the dance. Less formally, a person would sometimes dress up in two or three shirts and a number of robes and would then dance through the crowd, inviting people to take the clothing until he or she had nothing left. Occasionally someone would make an ostentatious gesture by raffling off an item of great value, gathering up little sticks and giving one to each of the people he or she wished to favor. The recipients later got together and gambled for the prize.[28]

Winter dances were held everywhere on the Plateau by both Salish and Sahaptin peoples. Most often, after one village in a given area held a dance, a nearby village would hold one, then another village, and then another. This resulted in a succession of spirit dances lasting up to two months. Some families would travel from link to link in the ceremonial chain for that entire period, returning home only when their enthusiasm waned.[29] With the end of the ceremonial season, the Plateau people, exhausted and elated, returned to their winter villages, where they resumed their more mundane winter activities until the migratory birds and hibernating animals reappeared and the annual round began once again.

Though this sounds like a simple and idyllic lifestyle, it was actually a very complex and well-managed system. In a highly varied and often marginal environment, extreme flexibility and intergroup cooperation were the only ways to ensure survival.

Each subgroup could be confident that the task group system would provide sufficient labor to make use of all of the resources within its territory. At the same time, because large population concentrations only formed while a task was being performed, there was less chance of overtaxing the area's resources or risking large-scale famine. Finally, there was so much variation between the Plateau's microenvironments that momentary disasters seldom affected the entire region. Thus the people could usually depend on finding food and other necessities even in the most extreme situations. For example, in a year when the salmon runs failed in the upper Columbia, a band on the lower reaches of the river could provide, through the structure of the task group system, either permission to use their fishing sites or dried fish or both.[30]

The task group system did not stop there, however. To the Plateau people, the earth was not just a provider of resources; it was the point of origin of all life. Being products of the earth, the resources that were harvested were not simply commodities, but living things with the same ultimate origin as the people themselves. As such, these things were also social beings possessed of souls, minds, and wills. Therefore, the commodities were also part of the task group system and very real members of the social community.[31]

Any given task group thus consisted of a human component, tied together through a complex set of social relations, and a nonhuman component, also tied through a complex set of social relations both to the human component and to other nonhuman entities. Seen in this way, it becomes clear that, as well structured and efficient as the task group system was, economic productivity was just its superficial purpose. At its heart, this system was designed to maintain proper social relations among all the entities on the Plateau, human, nonhuman, and superhuman. These social relations provided the substance of life and gave an identity to everything in the Plateau world.

Among aboriginal Plateau dwellers, identity in the sense of the isolated ego did not exist. Instead, the people derived their identities from the complex network of relationships that characterized the social structure. This is not to say that there was no sense of individual uniqueness among Plateau people, but individual identity was not isolated and intrinsic for them. Instead, uniqueness was acquired by interweaving threads of individual experience with the warp created by the many strands of relationships that formed the social world.[32]

The guardian spirit complex is an example of this integrated form of identity. The guardian spirit phenomenon provided four sources of individual identity for Plateau people. First, individuals were given unique spiritual qualities that manifested themselves in the form of specific skills. Second, the spirits demanded highly idiosyncratic behavior from their human partners. Third, each individual was given a name, a song, and a sacred bundle that was his or hers alone. Finally, no two individuals possessed the same spirit power in an identical form or to an identical degree. Just as no Plains warrior "was ever *as brave as* another, for each was brave in his own right," no Plateau person was ever *as spiritual as* another, for each was spiritual in his own right.[33]

As idiosyncratic and individualistic as these characteristics were, they were not intrinsic, nor did they exist in isolation. Even the most private aspects of the individual's identity were conceived as being the product of a social relationship. In addition, the identity that these spiritual relations conferred was not seen as being permanent. Relations between person and spirit evolved over time, making the core identity changeable.[34] Furthermore, while the person-spirit relationship formed the most basic element in the complex social structure, webs of identity-forming relationships radiated outward in both the human and nonhuman realms. As balances of spiritual power formed and dissolved, the person's relative power and identity changed. Hence, a very gifted fisherman might be accorded a special high-status identity during a time when spiritual interactions created a fish shortage, only to have that status altered when a new set of spiritual balances created a new situation.[35]

As the primary celebration of the guardian spirit phenomenon, the winter dance was the pivot for this complex social, economic, and psychological system. Through it, individuals and groups were able to join with the larger social world and reaffirm their membership. At the same time, through activities like spirit singing and dancing, it was possible to trace all of the connecting webs, reaffirming the relative identities of all of the Plateau dwellers, human and nonhuman alike.

On the practical level, by announcing the receipt of guardian spirits by its members and identifying the nature of these spirits, a group was asserting its particular economic strengths relative to the larger group. For example, if a band had a large number of people who were granted strong fishing powers, this would be its predominant activity in the task group system. In addition, the number of people who received spirits, and the strength of these spirits as revealed in competitions like the *toe-ya-khin*, helped to identify individuals and groups that were especially in tune with the immediate spiritual balance, thus most likely to play a leading role in economic and social life. Even such social activities as gift giving played a part in identifying the economic role of a host group. Not only did the giving of gifts indicate that a host band was capable of generating a surplus; the nature of the gifts (baskets, dried fish, etc.) identified the group's particular economic strengths. This information, combined with the unselfish generosity evidenced by large-scale gift giving, helped to fix the hosts' place in the immediate social and economic cosmos.

To the Plateau people, however, this was merely the most superficial level of a much more complicated matrix. All of these practical things were possible only because of the successful harmonizing of human and nonhuman beings and spirits. In this sense, the task group system was not a calculated subsistence strategy but a fully integrated system of beliefs and practices. It was a religion, and the Plateau community was a church in which every aspect of life was a sacrament.[36] Through membership in this church, every entity on the Plateau found a purpose and gained an identity.

By demanding a careful balance of assertiveness, ethics, and extreme adaptability, this system accommodated the individual to his or her place in the concentric rings of relationships that held the social cosmos together. That, in turn, permitted the unusual degree of intergroup cooperation that made the exploitation of a changeable habitat efficient and highly rewarding. Furthermore, by tying status and identity to the shifting economic and spiritual needs of the intersecting groups, this sytem made the emergence of permanent social classes and resulting conflicts of interest virtually impossible. Finally, and perhaps most important, this system, in conjunction with the powers and warnings provided by the guardian spirits and the knowledge stored in their encyclopedic repository of folklore, gave the Plateau people an unusual resiliency in the face of crisis. Within a few hundred years of the formation of this culture, however, a series of crises began that would eventually shatter the Plateau church and the Plateau world.

CHAPTER 2

The Eighteenth-Century Crisis

A mere 250 years after the Plateau culture had jelled, the system was threatened by a change so massive that it affected all of the environments that had been bridged by the task group system. This was the result of the Little Ice Age: a three-hundred-year cold spell.[1] Little research has been done on the specific influence of this climatic shift on Plateau weather patterns, but much can be extrapolated from more general studies. For example, Ellsworth Huntington's data on the growth rate of California sequoia trees suggests some broader trends. Increased growth rates are triggered by increased moisture and moderate temperatures. Extremes are detrimental, cold retarding a tree's biological functions and heat causing rapid evaporation and water deprivation.[2] By weighing these factors against the width of tree rings, he arrived at a fairly good general picture of past weather conditions in the Far West.

According to Huntington's figures, the giant trees enjoyed a major growing spurt beginning in 1551, corresponding to the onset of the Little Ice Age in Europe. The increased growth rate

23

continued uninterrupted for almost a century and a half until, in 1691, a decline to pre-1551 rates occurred. This was the beginning of four decades of relatively bad growth. Then, in 1731 another spurt began, which, with the exception of two isolated decades (1761–1770 and 1781–1790), continued unabated until 1891, when an even greater growing spurt took place.[3] This growth activity reveals a great deal about western American weather patterns. The sharp increase in tree growth that took place in 1551 indicates that the westerly air flow documented in Europe also affected the American West, bringing increased moisture from the Pacific onto the coast. Since the onshore westerly pattern was associated with a southward shift of the polar air mass, it must have been appreciably colder as well.[4]

A recent analysis of both tree ring data and pollen samples taken from the Columbia River area bears this out. According to Harold Fritts, G. Robert Lofgren, and Geoffrey A. Gordon, mean winter temperatures along the Pacific Northwest Coast were 0.3 degree centigrade colder during this period than at present, while further inland the temperature decline was 1.8 degrees. Concurrently, precipitation in the coastal area was a remarkable 8 percent higher than it is now.[5] Though the Rocky Mountain region was protected somewhat from this increased precipitation, the large gap carved by the Columbia River would have permitted the unusually moist westerly air flow to penetrate into the Plateau relatively unimpeded.

Though these figures may seem small, the environmental impact was undoubtedly enormous. Thompson Webb III has discovered that a sustained temperature change of 4 degrees accompanied by an 18-centimeter change in mean annual rainfall totally altered the natural environment between 10,000 and 11,000 years ago. He also discovered that a 1-degree depression of temperature that prevailed during the Little Ice Age had a profound effect on both plants and animals in the area he investigated.[6] The same was undoubtedly true on the Plateau, where the availability of the roots, nuts, and berries that composed a large portion of the aboriginal diet must thus have been reduced. Archaeological evidence provides some substantiation for this conclusion, for bison, pronghorn antelope, and mountain sheep disappeared entirely as food items in some areas during the critical years.[7]

With these foods absent or in short supply, salmon would have been an even more important source of nourishment than usual. Although archaeological evidence indicates that salmon were still present and being caught during the climatic crisis, they were probably not as abundant. Their upstream migration is retarded by floods and completely inhibited by extremely high water. During the Little Ice Age the increased precipitation and associated winter snowpack would have resulted in a spring runoff of significant volume, making the salmon runs either late or light and, in some years, probably nonexistent.[8]

That the Plateau people survived is a tribute to the task group system, with its totally integrated structure of economic cooperation. The worsened climate only threatened the quality of life, not life itself. These same cultural characteristics brought unprecedented prosperity when the climate improved at the beginning of the eighteenth century.[9] Between 1691 and 1730 the marked reduction in sequoia growth indicates that the polar storm track must have relocated slightly northward. The result would have been somewhat warmer and dryer weather, increasing the length and quality of the growing season and producing bumper crops of berries, roots, and meat. Also, since the spring runoff was reduced, heavy salmon runs would once again have penetrated deeply into the upper Columbia system.

To the Plateau people, the opening years of the eighteenth century must have seemed like a providential reprieve, but the relief was short-lived. The westerly flow resumed in 1731, keeping the weather consistently cold and wet until long after the aboriginal world had come to an end. The Plateau culture had survived the first 250 years of the Little Ice Age relatively unscathed, so there is no reason to believe that the ensuing bad years would have posed any major threat. But the return of this destructive climatic regime coincided with the arrival of a series of other equally destructive forces, the conjunction of which imperiled not only the culture but life itself.

While the Plateau people had been busy adapting to severe weather conditions, Europe was in the midst of an unprecedented period of expansion.[10] Though it would be centuries before white people came into direct contact with the Plateau Indians, the arrival of these strangers in Mexico and on the eastern seaboard sent waves of dislocation throughout North America. Conjoined with the return of bad weather, these waves created a general crisis on the Plateau during the eighteenth century.[11]

The first of these white-inspired waves to touch the Plateau was the horse frontier. The horse was introduced onto the Plateau about 1700, just as the climatic improvement was at its peak. Although the animals were being traded northward from Spanish settlements by 1630, this early trade did not progress very far. Two separate developments combined to increase the northward flow. First, the Pueblo Revolt in 1680 put large numbers of horses into Indian hands for the first time. Second, the climatic amelioration, beginning in 1691, provided weather far more appropriate for horse breeding. This fortuitous combination of increased supply and improved conditions permitted the veritable northward flood of horses in the early eighteenth century.[12]

The spread of horses from New Spain to the Plateau was a by-product of a major population shift. During the Little Ice Age the westerlies created a dry wedge of air that stretched from the eastern flank of the Rockies to the western fringe of the woodlands. In this area precipitation was reduced by 30–50 percent, destroying much of the vegetation. This forced agricultural Plains dwellers to desert their normal habitat and take up new residences in the East.[13] While these Caddoan and other Plains farmers were withdrawing, desert-adapted Numic speakers flooded into the area. Linguistic evidence indicates that the Numic branch of the larger Uto-Aztecan language family had slowly drifted north and east from their original Great Basin homeland until about A.D. 100, at which time they occupied an area on the fringe of the Plateau. D. B. Shimkin puts this Numic cultural center between the Snake River, the Uintah River, and the Wind River Mountains. This group, in turn, fractured into several parts, eventually forming such disparate "tribes" as the Shoshoni, Ute, Paiute, and Comanche. Though divided linguistically and politically, these related groups eventually invaded and occupied the whole of the western Plains from the southwestern desert to Montana, creating a chain of kinship and trade through which the horses passed. It was through this chain that the Plateau people got their horses.[14]

The horse was a bio-invader in an environment where there were few natural predators and in which conditions for both forage and breeding were ideal. The horse population increased from a few scattered herds to immense numbers in one century. The Plateau people were forced to make numerous cultural adjustments in order to make productive use of the animal.[15] Their semisedentary flexibility had to give way to a new pastoral lifestyle. For example, because horses permitted hunters to penetrate farther into the mountains after game and to bring back larger loads of meat, the fall hunts acquired added importance. Horses also changed the locations of fall hunting camps from the high, rocky slopes to sites nearer the alpine meadows where grazing was available.[16]

More significant, buffalo hunting became a regular part of the annual round. The horse made it unnecessary for the *khoo-say-nee* to abandon their homes to become migratory buffalo hunters. By decreasing the travel time, the horse made it possible for Plateau hunting parties to venture to the Yellowstone or other hunting sites and back every fall. Furthermore, since horses could carry heavier loads than could either women or their dogs, it was possible to bring the meat back home. As a result, buffalo consumption increased noticeably, as did the volume of buffalo by-products used in intertribal trade.[17] In turn, the increased volume of food and trade goods enhanced the purchasing power and status of buffalo-hunting groups and the entire Plateau community in interareal relations. This, combined with the trade value of the horses themselves, ensured far greater economic power and flexibility. Such economic benefits became particularly important when the Little Ice Age recommenced, making the ability to draw on all possible economic resources a necessity. The horse then provided a welcome counterweight to the deteriorating climate.

For all of the benefits the horse contributed to Plateau life, it also exacted a cost. Because the Plateau people were on the horse frontier, they found themselves the victims of violent avarice, which was, however, only one part of a much larger process. Several other moving frontiers combined with the appeal of horses to create an environment in which violence became an unavoidable aspect of the accepted order. In the middle of the seventeenth century, population waves generated by the European penetration of the Atlantic seaboard moved across the continent. Propelled by white population pressure and the exigencies of the fur trade, the Iroquois and Chippewa pushed westward, bringing death and destruction with them. Caddoans, Siouans and Great Lakes Algonkians were gradually pushed onto the Plains. Further north, the Blackfeet were shoved out of the woods onto the plains of Saskatchewan.[18]

It was not long before the Numic Plains peoples began to feel the pressure, but their mastery of the horse, combined with their early adaptation to the desiccated environment, gave them an immediate military advantage. Instead of being on the defensive, these Numic speakers defeated the newcomers easily, winning war captives who were traded for horses and manufactured items in New Mexico.[19] This superiority was not to last. If the demand for territory was not enough to prompt a challenge to the Numic peoples' power, the fact that they raided for captives continuously and on a large scale was. By raiding indiscriminately, these people alienated everyone around them. This common threat overrode traditional animosities among the Eastern tribes and gave rise to a defensive coalition of Blackfeet, Sarcee, Atsina, Assiniboin, and Plains Cree that might be called the Eastern Alliance. These tribes objected to such cavalier treatment at the hands of the mounted Numics and began raiding back, concentrating on acquiring horses and the technology that went with them. As this strategy paid off, the alliance became increasingly offensive until, by the 1750s, they were beginning to push the Numic speakers back.[20]

It was at this point that the Plateau people entered into the situation. By the 1750s they had mastered the horse and had added Plains hunting to their annual round, which brought them into the continuing battle for possession of the buffalo lands. More significant, however, violence was being brought home to the Plateau itself. Though the Plateau tribes maintained friendly relations with many neighboring Numic bands, their relations with the more southern Shoshoni, centering around the eventual site of Fort Hall, were poor. These Snake Indians and their allies, the Bannock, raided the relatively defenseless Plateau people in their quest for captives, and the raids increased as the Eastern Allies grew more adept at defending themselves.[21]

Although the Plateau people had fewer arms and horses, they did their best to make the Plateau seem less desirable, waging unceasing war on the invaders. Even so, the Snake continued to launch sporadic slave raids and forays for weapons and vengeance.[22] The result was something of a balance of power. Neither the Plateau people, the Snake, nor the Eastern Alliance was strong enough to overcome either of the others. Sovereignty over the northwestern Plains remained uncertain as each of the three groups continued to hunt in the area and fight to control it. Sporadic raiding and running battles became common, but the balance of power was effective insurance against annihilation.[23]

Unfortunately for all concerned, the balance of power did not last long. The threat of Numic raiders was all that had held the Eastern Alliance together, and by the mid-1770s that was a thing of the past. In addition, continuing white pressure and the unsettling influence of colonial warfare resulted in further waves of resettlement among Atlantic and Midwestern Indians and brought increased westward pressures to bear on the Blackfeet and their erstwhile allies. Also, because of their frontier position, the Blackfeet had acquired the greatest wealth of horses among the Eastern Allies, making them a target of acquisitive jealousy. The Eastern Alliance foundered under these strains and finally disintegrated.[24]

Thereupon the Blackfeet, the former shock troops of the Eastern Alliance, became the victims of their neighbors' need for horses. As Alexander Henry the elder observed, the Assiniboin organized raids on their former allies consisting of "greater numbers than can be counted, armed with bow, sling and spear, and with quivers full of arrows"—and, after Henry's visit, with guns, powder, and ball.[25] The pressure exerted by such repeated shows of force compelled the Blackfeet to relocate again. In a matter of one generation the Piegan Blackfeet moved from central Saskatchewan to the eastern foot of the Rockies, where they carved out a new, though much disputed, homeland for themselves. This put them at the precise point of convergence between the rapidly merging horse and gun frontiers.[26]

Working in their favor was the fact that the Blackfeet maintained friendly relations with at least some tribes who had access to firearms. One of these was the Gros Ventre. Located near the center of the western fur trade, this tribe was well provided with both guns and ammunition but had a great desire for horses and captives. From them, huge amounts of goods flooded west. Fur trader Charles Mackenzie once observed the Gros Ventre selling two hundred guns and two thousand rounds of ammunition along with a hundred bushels of corn and a number of white "mercantile articles" in a single transaction.[27]

This gave the Blackfeet a powerful motive for raiding on the Plateau. Their situation demanded that they acquire more horses, and they were well aware that the Flathead, Kutenai, Pend d'Oreille, and Nez Perce owned the best animals. Their military superiority over the Plateau people also allowed them to take female and juvenile captives who could be sold as slaves.[28] Adding to the appeal of these commodities was the Plateau peoples' relative inability to defend them. As Alexander Henry the younger observed of the Blackfeet, "They are perpetually at war with the Snakes, Flat Heads, and other nations, who have vast herds, and who appear to be a defenseless race; having no firearms."[29] In this way, the Blackfeet temporarily insured their continued existence.

The continued existence of the Plateau people was not so certain, however. The first to feel the pressure were the tribes that resided on the eastern flank of the mountains: the Flathead and the Tuna'xe, or Eastern Kutenai. In the face of this pressure the Tuna'xe were wiped out and the Flatheads were forced to retire to the west side of the mountains. Unfortunately, as soon as the Blackfeet had swept the Plateau people over to the west of the Continental Divide, they began to raid there as well.[30]

To make matters worse, by the 1770s competition between the Hudson's Bay Company and various other trading outfits had pushed the fur trade all the way to the Rockies.[31] Although they were a pivotal part of this trade, it is interesting to note that the Blackfeet were not a good source for beaver pelts. Charles Mackenzie explained, "They consider the operation of searching for them in the bowels of the earth, to satisfy the avarice of the Whites, not only troublesome, but very degrading."[32] Hence they refused to do more than dabble in the fur trade and were often threatening and abusive even then. Considering the Blackfoot attitude and the paltry returns, the fur traders did not find spending time in the war-torn northern Plains worth the risk.[33]

The fur traders chose instead to concentrate on the more peaceful and productive regions of the Far North. There was one major drawback to this strategy, however. While the subarctic supplied plenty of furs, it could provide almost no food for those who hunted them. According to trader W. F. Wentzel, food was so scarce during one winter that he was forced to eat the beaver skins he had taken in trade.[34] Although they controlled great wealth, the fur companies could not afford to have their profits eaten up in this way, and this compelled them to look for a source of provisions for their northern brigades.

They found this source in the vast buffalo herds that ranged across Blackfoot country. The value of this food source more than compensated the traders for the risks involved in entering the intertribal war zone. Furthermore, the Blackfeet loved to hunt buffalo and found trading in that commodity anything but degrading, making the so-called *Gens du Large* less threatening to their white trading partners. As Mackenzie pointed out, "They often remark to me that they would think it a pleasure to supply us with beavers if they could be secured the same as buffaloes by a chase on horseback."[35] Here was the opportunity, and the accompanying pleasure was compounded by the fact that the Blackfeet could get guns, ammunition, and other white commodities.

Given a task they liked, the Blackfeet became extremely productive. In his 31 January 1795 report from Fort George, Duncan M'Gillivray was able to communicate to his North West Company employers that

> upon examining the Warehouses it appears that our trade amounts to . . . 8900 lb Pounded meat with at least a sufficient quantity of fat to employ it, so that however deficient we may be in Packs at the embarkation, there is every appearance that the quantity of provisions will answer the expectations of the Gentn. of the Northern Posts, who depend on us for this necessary article.[36]

By spring the amount of pounded meat was up to 10,000 pounds, and this was less than half of the meat traded in the area. According to M'Gillivray, the nearby Hudson's Bay Company post was far more popular with the Blackfeet and received the lion's share of the business.[37]

M'Gillivray never commented on how much the *Gens du Large* were paid for their labors except to say that they were "treated with less liberality" than were beaver hunters. Still, it was enough to upset the balance of power between the Plain tribes and the Plateau people. As M'Gillivray pointed out, the newly acquired wealth of arms and ammunition was "rendered valuable by the great advantage it gives them in their expeditions to the Rocky Mountains."[38] Considering the Indian meat monopoly and the huge volume of that commodity consumed by the fur traders, the advantage must have grown rapidly.

The only course left open for the Plateau people was to attempt to break through the Blackfeet and get involved in the trade. They did not wait long. In a journal entry dated 22 February 1795, M'Gillivray reported that

the Coutonees [Koutenai] a tribe from the Southwest are determined to force their way this year to the Fort or perish in the attempt. . . . The Gens du Large and all the other nations in this
neighborhood wishing to retain an exclusive trade among themselves, have hitherto prevented the Intentions of this Band, of
commencing a friendly intercourse with the Fort, in order to ex-
clude them from any share of our commodities, which they are
well aware would put their enemies in a condition to defend
themselves, from the attacks of those who are already acquainted
with the use of arms. The Coutonees have already made several
attempts to visit us, but they have been always obstructed by their
enemies and forced to relinquish their design with loss:—this
year however it is reported that they intend obtaining a safe passage hither by bribing their enemies with Bands of Horses.
Whether this method will succeed we cannot judge, but it is
shrewdly suspected that a party will be formed to intercept as
usual their progress to this quarter.[39]

Since M'Gillivray never reported their arrival it may be assumed
that the outcome he so "shrewdly suspected" actually came to
pass.

With this northern trade corridor blocked, the Plateau people
found themselves looking for alternative sources for arms and
other goods. Coincidentally, the Crow, hoping to open a trade
conduit between the Plateau tribes and the Missouri, were then
advancing from the east.[40] The resulting conduit between the
horse and gun frontiers did not, however, bring salvation. Instead, it may have brought more death and destruction to the
Plateau than both horses and guns put together.

A disease frontier moved across America in virulent waves
during the sixteenth and seventeenth centuries.[41] Though
we have no record of the earliest Plains epidemics, they probably followed the same northward course as the horse. If so,
the Numic peoples would have borne the brunt of the infec-
tion, which may have contributed to their downfall during the
eighteenth century. In the first major epidemic for which we do
have evidence, a group of these people were the carriers of the

disease. In a letter to Samuel Hearne, Mathew Cocking reported that

> some of the Indians who went to war last year having met with a Tent of Snake Indians who were ill of the Small Pox, they killed and Skalped them, by this means they received the disorder themselves, and most of them died on their return, the few that reached their own Parts communicated the Disorder to their Countrymen and since then it has run with great rapidity through the whole Country above here and is now raging.[42]

Rage it did, wreaking devastation across the Great Plains. William Tomison, reporting from Cumberland House in February 1782, stated:

> We have buried Upwards of 30 for Which Number there is only two recovered & they are but Children, the U,Basquiau Indians are all Dead & ten tents of Pegogemy and Cowintou Indians that was Pitching towards this place all Died, as to all those that went up the Sturgeon River, I have neither seen nor heard from them since they had Debt last Autumn. My Trade near 4000 made Beaver, but I do not know where there is any more to come from, as my Debtors are all Dead. I have about 1000 beaver out in Debts, which I believe will be all lost by Death.[43]

Like their neighbors, the Crow contracted the disease and spread it wherever they went, which, by the end of the eighteenth century, included the Plateau. Here, the survivors of Blackfoot aggression succumbed to the pox by the thousands. According to anthropologist James Teit,

> The survivors [of the intertribal wars] were nearly all swept off by small pox about 1800. The Flathead are said to have been reduced to nearly half at the same time. The disease is said to have come from the Crow, passed through the Flathead to the Semte'use, Pend d'Oreilles, and Kalispel, and on to the Spokan and Colville, eventually dying out among the Salish tribes of the Columbia River. The Sahaptian tribes are said to have escaped or to have been only slightly affected. The Pend d'Oreilles, Kalispel, and Spokan, Colville and Columbia all suffered severely, but the disease is said to have been worst among the Spokan, whole bands of whom were wiped out.[44]

This epidemic was followed by many more, as measles and other contagious diseases were transmitted from a number of sources and joined smallpox in spreading death. The first federal Indian agent in the Northwest, Elijah White, bore witness to the devastation, reporting in 1845 that as best as he could estimate, the native population of the region had declined from five hundred thousand to twenty-seven thousand since 1800, a reduction of over 94 percent in less than fifty years.[45]

Epidemic disease was merely the last of the many destructive waves that swept across the land in the eighteenth century, but it was the most devastating of the lot. The conjunction of sickness with the coming of horses, guns, climatic deterioration, and near constant war put an unbearable strain on the Plateau world. In response, the Plateau people abandoned many of their most treasured ideals, including the concepts of equality and parochialism, in exchange for a chance at survival.

CHAPTER 3

The Plateau Prophecy

Before the eighteenth-century crisis, the Plateau task group system had molded a multiplicity of parochial villages into a number of fluidly structured larger groups. Through the winter dance complex, these were forged into a single church that provided a meaningful core for the Plateau world. Because of its profound impact on so many aspects of life, the crisis shook this system to its foundations.

The autonomy of local villages had begun to erode in the early eighteenth century. Before that time, large-scale organizations had been limited both by the distance between villages and, more important, by the limited availability of resources. The arrival of the horse minimized these limitations. First, the perceived distance between groups was reduced, while the speed and reliability of communication were increased. Also, the range of exploitable territory was expanded. At the same time, the arrival of a temporarily improved climate increased the yield of existing economic resources. Each of these developments expanded the potential size of political groups, permitting a large

37

number of people to move as a unit for the first time.[1] This ability to move as a unit was especially valuable considering the new economic activities, particularly buffalo hunting, forced upon the Plateau people by radically changing conditions and became a strong influence when the Little Ice Age recommenced, making such activities a necessity.[2]

The demand for consolidation was also enhanced by the demographic disasters wreaked by the ever encroaching disease frontier. In a nonagricultural economy in which cooperative effort was demanded, the decline of suppliers also created a decline in supplies. Therefore the precipitous reduction in population left the scattered bands unable to defend themselves or to exploit the economic resources they needed to survive.[3] In the midst of such a disaster, the sacrifice of local autonomy must have seemed a small price to pay for the security of group support.

In addition, the meeting of the horse and gun frontiers combined with a shared economic investment in the buffalo plains to create a persistent state of war. This violent environment led the fur trader Alexander Ross to observe, "These Indians, with all their independence, are far from being happy people. They live in a constant state of anxiety. Every hostile movement about the frontier excites alarm and sets the whole country on the *qui vive*."[4] With the people scattered across the country in disease-wracked autonomous bands, however, being on the *qui vive* was not enough: defense required unified action. So, as Spinden said of the Nez Perce, "the necessity of a united defense against invading war-parties from the Plains probably brought about . . . tribal integrity."[5] The Nez Perce was not the only group so affected. In his 1849 report, explorer Charles Wilkes commented on similar organizational upheavals among the Eastern Salish. Similar developments have also been noted among the Flathead, Cayuse, Coeur d'Alene, Umatilla, Kutenai, Pend d'Oreille, Spokan, and Kalispel, all of whom were involved with the Nez Perce in raiding and buffalo hunting.[6]

The need for defense and the increasing need for centralization called for a greater degree of leadership and discipline than had been acceptable to Plateau peoples traditionally. They met this organizational need by creating two coexisting governments, each with exclusive jurisdiction within its specific area. Their leadership needs they met by scrapping the traditional egalitarian system and adopting a new social regime.

The first of these two co-governments was the direct result of the Plateau peoples' military needs and was responsible for warfare and diplomacy. This government centered around the war chief, a man chosen from a newly dominant social class of warriors. In the old days, war skills had been of relatively little significance, but with the emergence of the new situation on the Plateau, military skill and bravery eclipsed most other gifts, and the status of warriors increased accordingly. In fact, after the middle of the eighteenth century, a man's war record became the primary means of fixing his social ranking.[7]

Another major distortion in the sociopolitical system was related even more closely to the horse. Before the introduction of this animal, Plateau society viewed property as subject to group stewardship. Salmon-fishing or deer-hunting sites belonged to the group, and the proceeds of the site's use were shared among its members. The horse, however, needed more than just a place to live; it needed supervision. This promoted the concept of individual control. Because of the importance of the horse to the welfare of the group at large, those who were particularly gifted horse breeders and caretakers were granted increased status in the group.[8]

Horses did not constitute wealth in the European sense, but they did resemble modern capital in some significant ways. First, horse herds were highly visible, so one's relative standing in the community was constantly on display. Second, herds grew in direct proportion to their initial size, so the more one had to begin with, the faster one could produce more. Finally, horses were directly inheritable. Aided by these characteristics and the fact that the horse continued to be a widely valued commodity until well into the current century, those who possessed large herds came to form an aristocracy.

It was from this newly emerged aristocracy that the other demand for leadership was met. The second arm of the government was based on the leadership of locally prominent headmen who were responsible for domestic issues, arbitrated local disputes, and provided direction and general goals for the group. Traditionally these men had been chosen for their social prestige, which depended on the whole complex of inter- and intragroup relations and the peoples' immediate needs. The fixed nature of horse-derived status changed this so that the new aristocracy gained control of these local government positions. This power was then further enhanced by intermarriage with other chiefly families, resulting in a strong leadership base.[9]

There was little or no friction between the civil and military governments or their leaders. The functions of each arm were carefully differentiated so that there could not be much conflict. Also, war leaders frequently came from the aristocratic class or, through successful horse stealing, ended up there. Furthermore, the practice of intermarriage between chiefly families created a community of interest that ensured political consistency and aided greatly in the continuing centralization process. As a result, a tribal consciousness developed and took its place beside already powerful local and task group consciousness.

While it would be tempting to hypothesize that the emergence of tribal consciousness should have strained the pattern of mutual cooperation and co-participation in ceremonial and economic activities, the opposite seems to have been the case. It would appear that greater tribal rigidity added strength to the intertribal task group system and that a more or less formal league or confederacy emerged among the Plateau peoples. As Ray proposed, there were several leagues of similar tribes that, because they were fairly small and tended to emphasize local autonomy in their domestic arrangements, needed such an organization for the larger scale economic, ceremonial, and military tasks imposed by the new crisis-inspired situation. Apparently the Wenatchi, Kittitas, Klickitat, Yakima, Walula, Nez Perce, Spokan, and Colville were all tribes around which local leagues were centered. As before, the orbits surrounding each of these focal groups intersected at several points, retaining the complicated web of relations that held the Plateau together.[10]

Undoubtedly the need for mutual defense from raiding Plains tribes was instrumental in forging strong links between tribes, but other forces were also important. First, the emergence of stronger tribal organizations required that the structure for dealing with area-wide problems also be strengthened, if conflict was to be avoided. This process was no doubt exacerbated by the emergence of a chiefly faction whose sole responsibility was diplomatic relations.[11] More important, about the same time that Plains raiding began, the climatic amelioration came to an end, reducing the salmon runs, game populations, and vegetable harvests once again. The renewed need for economic cooperation undoubtedly enhanced the strengthening of bonds.

None of the changes in Plateau life were the result of cultural intrusion. They were, instead, the product of cultural distortion brought on by dynamic pressures from outside. These pressures and the changes they caused turned many central aspects of Plateau culture upside down. Under such conditions, the delicate balance between the physical and the spiritual worlds could not have continued undisturbed. Therefore, the pressures exerted by outside forces combined with the pressures created by cultural change to require the formation of a new thought pattern that could bring some order to the changing scene.[12]

According to psychological anthropologist Anthony F. C. Wallace, for a society to be stable, each member must "maintain a mental image of the society and its culture, as well as of his own body and its behavioral regularities, in order to act in ways which reduce stress at all levels of the system." He calls this complex mental image the "mazeway" because,

> as a model of the cell-body-personality-nature-culture-society system, or field, organized by the individual's own experiences, it includes perceptions of both the maze of physical objects of the environment (internal and external, human and nonhuman) and also of the ways in which this maze can be manipulated by the self and others in order to minimize stress. The mazeway is nature, society, culture, personality, and body image, as seen by one person.[13]

If increasing amounts of stress are brought to bear on the members of a given society, the mazeway is increasingly taxed in its function of dissipating the stress throughout the organism. In an effort to reduce the building stress, changes may be made in surface elements of the culture, but, because these do not alter the basic mazeway, the result is merely distortion and increased anxiety.

Eventually, the rising level of stress and the decreasing ability to cope force an unavoidable decision between maintaining the present mazeway and tolerating the stress, or changing the mazeway to try to reduce the stress. Any number of forces could work together to prompt a change in mazeway. Wallace lists "climatic, floral, and faunal change; military defeat, political subordination; extreme pressure toward acculturation resulting in internal cultural conflict; economic distress; epidemics, and so on."[14] Once the system reaches the point where stress can no longer be relieved or tolerated, Wallace continues, the entire system has to be scrapped. While some traditional elements of the culture may remain the same, they and all of reality come to be seen in a new and revolutionary way: a way that helps to diffuse stress rather than concentrate it.[15]

This is precisely what took place on the Plateau. Although the cultural changes I have discussed helped the Plateau people to survive the initial meeting of the various frontiers, without a change in mazeway these changes were distortions and only enhanced anxiety. As the climatic change and other natural forces added more stress to the already overstressed society, it finally reached its breaking point and had to forge a new metaphysical arrangement. The Plateau Prophets were born.[16]

A lack of documentary evidence makes it difficult to fix the date at which the aboriginal mazeway broke down. One event that helps to date the phenomenon, however, is the arrival of the "dry snow." According to a Spokan Indian named Silimxnotylmilakobok, when he was about ten years old he was awakened by his mother, who told him that the world was ending. He then heard what sounded like a great peal of thunder. "Something was falling very thick," he continued. At first the people believed that it was snowing, but upon going outside, they discovered that ashes were falling. These fell to a depth of 6 inches, causing them to imagine that the world was really coming to an end.[17]

Current residents of this area would immediately recognize this awe-inspiring phenomenon as a volcanic ashfall.

It is impossible to say whether or not this volcanic activity was the final change that overloaded the mazeway, but there is no question that prophet dance performances were associated with it. Like the Spokan, the Nespelem were much alarmed, fearing the ashfall prognosticated evil:

> They beat drums and sang, and for a time held the "praying" dance almost day and night. They prayed to the "dry snow," calling it "Chief" and "Mystery," and asked it to explain itself and tell why it came. The people danced a great deal all summer, and in large measure neglected their usual work. They put up only small stores of berries, roots, salmon, and dried meat; and consequently the following winter, which happened to be rather long and severe, they ran out of supplies. A few of the old people died of starvation and others became so weak that they could not hunt.[18]

This, according to a Nespelem informant, was the first time that a religious dance other than the winter guardian spirit dance had ever been held.[19]

Wilkes reported that Silimxnotylmilakobok dated the ashfall to fifty years before his telling of the tale, or about 1791. Teit's informants placed the date a bit earlier, closer to 1770, whereas Ray's sources claimed that it did not take place until 1800. If the dry snow was the trigger for the prophet cult, then the breakdown of the Plateau mazeway must have come during this thirty-year period. This is consistent with several Okanagon sources that date their prophet dance from the opening years of the nineteenth century or somewhat earlier. The time span is also in line with a Yakima tradition that traces their prophet experience to a smallpox epidemic that has been dated to 1782.[20]

Given the radical theology announced by the Prophets, it seems perfectly natural that the new religion may have been spurred by cataclysmic vulcanism. Until the dry snow fell, the Plateau people had believed that the world had always existed and would continue to exist forever.[21] Suddenly, in the face of one of nature's most powerful instruments for both creation and destruction, the Prophets announced a novel creed in which a newly conceived supernatural being called Chief had, with Coyote's assistance, created the world and predestined its end. According to this new theology, once everything had been created and was working right, Chief had sent Coyote away and told the people:

> "I will send messages to earth by the souls of people that reach me, but whose time to die has not yet come. They will carry messages to you from time to time; and when their souls return to their bodies, they will revive, and tell you their experiences. Coyote and myself will not be seen again until the Earth-Woman is very old. Then we shall return to earth, for it will require a new change by that time. Coyote will precede me by some little time; and when you see him, you will know the time is at hand. When I return, all spirits of the dead will accompany me, and after that there will be no spirit land. All the people will live together. Then will the Earth-Woman revert to her natural shape, and live as a mother among her children. Then things will be made right, and there will be much happiness."[22]

The messengers mentioned by Chief were the Prophets, from whom the complex got it name. All of these Prophets dreamed that they had visited the land of the dead and had spoken with Chief, who entrusted them with messages to be imparted to the people.[23]

The process for carrying out this mission undoubtedly varied among the many different groups, but the behavior of the Southern Okanagon was probably fairly typical. Among this group, the Prophet made it known that he had had a vision experience and invited the inhabitants of his village to his house. He would then describe his conversation with Chief, would predict a speedy end of the world, and would tell his audience that at a specific hour they would see a messenger from Chief who would call them forth to dance. At the stated time, the people, wearing no paint or special clothing nor bearing any ceremonial paraphernalia, would gather outside in a circle around the Prophet. Then the messenger would appear and the people would begin to dance, remaining in the circle but neither revolving nor changing their positions and singing a prayer song taught them by the Prophet. Each such event including a properly performed dance hastened the eventuality of the happy apocalypse.[24] Happier days were also hastened by proper moral behavior. As the cultural distortion process had taken place, traditional moral standards and means of communicating them had broken down. Chief therefore insisted that the Prophets impart a rigid code of behavior to ensure continual internal harmony in the face of external stress.[25]

With the mazeway thus restructured, the adaptations to the hostile environment of the late eighteenth century ceased to be appended anomalies and dropped into the mainstream of Plateau life. The society was literally "born again" and moved on as if the old ways had never existed. Certain old patterns were retained, but, like reality itself, they took on different meanings.

One of the first matters to be faced by this revitalized society was the enlargement of its network of relationships. Recognizing the need for "horse" Indians to unite against "gun" Indians, the Plateau people attempted to form a coalition with the Snake. Though this union was certainly in the best interests of both groups, much stood in its way. Even so, the Plateau people sent a peace delegation to the Snake in the summer of 1805, presumably to convert them and involve them in the Plateau congregation. Apparently, the Snake were not convinced: the peacemakers were executed in their camp. There followed a bloody war of vengeance.[26]

Though things looked bleak, the Prophets promised that a solution was on it way. According to Silimxnotylmilakobok, in addition to everything else that had happened when the dry snow had fallen, the Spokan Prophet had proclaimed, "Soon there will come from the rising sun a different kind of man from any you have yet seen, who will bring with them a book and will teach you everything, and after that the world will fall to pieces."[27] This vision was confirmed by Prophets throughout the Plateau. One, a Nez Perce, reported this information to the powerful war chief Hohots Ilppilp, warning him that these strangers would come from the land of their enemies, but if they stopped and smoked with the great war chief there would be peace.[28]

On 20 September 1805 the prophecy began to come true. On that day an advance party from the Lewis and Clark Expedition stumbled onto the Nez Perce portion of the Plateau. After pausing with some root gatherers, William Clark, who was commanding the advance force, led the small party to a village headed by a civil chief named Walammotinin. The headman told the explorers that he had heard of their coming and had sent messengers out to the other villages to invite the leading men to come and speak with the strangers. On 23 September, village heads from the Kamiah band of the Nez Perce came to Walammotinin's village for the interview. After these chiefs had arrived, they assembled with the explorers and all smoked together. The explorer then "informed them where we came from where bound our wish to inculcate peace and good understanding between all the red people &c."[29]

Though Lewis and Clark stayed among the Nez Perce for nineteen days, the Indians did not allow them to open official relations. Since this was a major development for the Plateau people, no official action could be taken until representatives from all the Plateau groups could assemble, but because of the war with the Snake, most of the important men were unavailable. Since the explorers could not wait and still make it to the Pacific by winter, it was decided that they would leave their horses with the Nez Perce and proceed immediately by boat.[30]

After completing their heroic transcontinental trek and wintering on the Pacific, the explorers returned to Walammotinin's village on the Plateau in early May 1806. From there they were accompanied by an honor guard of Plateau warriors led by a major Nez Perce council member named Neesh-ne-park-ke-ook to the village of a powerful leader named Tin-nach-e-moot-oolt. On 10 May, camps were set up for the whites and Indians near this village; its council lodge was to be used for the negotiations.

Meanwhile, Indians from all over the Plateau were also gathering. On the same day that Lewis and Clark arrived at the meeting place, Hohots Ilppilp arrived at the site with fifty village heads. The explorers were then told that a council was convening to speak to them in the name of the Nez Perce Nation and that the proceedings would begin as soon as one more council member arrived. At eight o'clock on the following morning, the last great chief, Yoom-park-kar-tim, arrived, the pipe was passed, and the session began.[31]

No minutes were kept of the Americans' presentation to the council, but Meriwether Lewis wrote a summary of what was said. According to his journal entry for 11 May 1806, the explorers went "minutely into the views of our government with respect to the inhabitants of this Western part of the Continent, their intentions of establishing trading houses for their relief, their wish to restore peace and harmony among the natives, the strength, wealth and powers of our nation &c."[32] This outline resembles a prepared speech Clark carried with him that emphasized the availability of guns and other useful items, the desire that the Indians live in peace, the American objective of establishing forts along the Missouri, and the prosperity of all the tribes that had "opened their ears" to the counsel of the United States government.[33]

This gave the Nez Perce and their allies everything they could want. The whites wanted the Plateau people to get along with their neighbors, a long-standing problem for which the Indians had been seeking a solution for some time. There had been the disastrous overture to the Snake. Now, if the newcomers kept their promises, the Plateau tribes would get sufficient support and arms to defend themselves from Snake raiders. Furthermore, unlike the Spanish, upon whom the Shoshoneans depended for white goods, the Americans did not seem interested in Indian slaves. Thus alliance with the Americans through the Plateau people would take care of the Snake's needs and eliminate the major impetus for their raiding activity.[34]

There was also the chance that the Blackfeet might see the advantages in making peace with the Plateau people. This seemed possible since, if all of Lewis and Clark's promises were kept, the Blackfeet would suddenly find themselves at a disadvantage in the new power structure. Though the Plateau spokesman held out this hope, he did not feel that such an occurrence was very likely. Just in case, however, the Indians resolved to send with the expedition three men who would negotiate with the enemy if they could. If not, they would return and warn the tribe to, as Clark put it, "remain on their guard with rispect to them untill the whites had it in their power to give them more effectual relief."[35]

It is no surprise, then, that the Plateau people heartily accepted the explorers' proposals. As Lewis paraphrased the tribal orator's response, "he observed that they had listened with attention to our advice and that the whole nation were resolved to follow it, that they had only one heart and one tongue on this subject. They were poor, but their hearts were good."[36] Things began to fall into place almost immediately. On 6 June, Tinnach-e-moot-oolt informed Clark that the Snake had arrived among the Cayuse and wanted to make peace with the whites and with all of the Plateau tribes.[37] Although negotiations were not conducted immediately, the explorers learned on 23 June that a peace had been negotiated successfully, allying the Snake with the Plateau confederacy.[38]

This was to be the only successful outcome of the Plateau-American arrangement. As both the whites and the Indians expected, the Americans were less than successful in negotiating with the Blackfeet. Though Lewis used all of his persuasive abilities in trying to bring about peace between these traditional enemies, his effort was completely in vain. The morning after his speech, the Blackfeet attacked the explorers while they slept. In the resulting melee, one Blackfoot was killed and another wounded, leaving little possibility for negotiating a treaty.[39]

That might not have been disastrous had the promise of trading posts in the buffalo country been kept. Unfortunately, Jeffersonian enthusiasm for this subtle approach to the Indian problem in the Far West was not shared by those directly responsible for Indian policy. Of the $921,775.26 appropriated for the factory system between 1789 and 1819, only $569,272.31

was actually spent, most of it east of the Mississippi. Only one government factory had been established as far west as the Missouri River by the time the system was officially disbanded in 1822. Located forty miles south of the present site of Kansas City, this one factory was certainly in no position to lend the Plateau tribes any "effectual relief."[40]

The Americans' failure to establish the promised far western factories robbed the Plateau strategy of its critical ingredient. The Plateau people were left to face increased Blackfoot hostility unarmed and without the military support they had anticipated. Without government posts as a source of inexpensive white goods, the Snake were forced to return to the Spanish and to slave raiding to supply their needs. Since the Plateau people remained the best target, friction between the two continued to increase until 1808, when a full-scale war broke out between the ex-allies.[41] Worse, the Blackfeet stepped up their offensive behavior. Lewis and Clark's penetration into the Far West raised fears among the Blackfeet that American goods might bypass the blockade that had closed the Canadian trade corridor so effectively. In a last-ditch effort to keep guns out of Plateau hands, the Blackfeet shifted their attention southward, launching attacks against both the Plateau Indians and white traders.[42]

Thus, instead of leading to the happy times promised in prophecy, Lewis and Clark's arrival on the Plateau appears only to have raised false hopes and worsened conditions. Actually, that was not quite the case. Prophecies seldom work themselves out in the most straightforward manner, and this one was no exception. Though it was perhaps imperceptible to the principals involved, everything was going according to Chief's plan. After all, Lewis and Clark had not been carrying a book to the Indians, thus they were not the harbingers of the millennium. They were, however, advance agents whose visit triggered the complicated process of completion by turning the Blackfeet's attention southward. That helped to open a trade corridor to the Plateau via the defiles of the Saskatchewan River. The North West Company's enterprising trader-explorer David Thompson took advantage of the opening in the spring of 1807 and sneaked across the mountains to build the first trading post on the Plateau itself.[43]

Thompson's presence on the Plateau marked a new era in the region's history. From a practical standpoint, his presence brought to fruition all of the Plateau people's diplomatic and trade strategies. In building Kutenai House and the posts that followed, Thompson provided the direct trade for which they had been striving. He also played the pacifying role they had hoped the Americans would perform. More important than diplomacy and trade, however, was the spiritual significance of Thompson's arrival. Like many of his co-workers, Thompson was a practicing Christian, and his penetration into the area brought the final phase of the prophecy into operation.[44]

CHAPTER 4

The Prophecy Unfolds

The Plateau people were fully aware of Thompson's role in the unfolding of the prophecy, and there was great rejoicing following his arrival. During an extended tour of the Northwest in 1811, Thompson received almost the same greeting at every Plateau stop.[1] At his initial stopping place, he smoked and ate with the assembled village and then asked to see the Indians dance. He reported that, in response to his request, the chief of the village

> made a short speech to them, and all of them, young and old men, women and children, began to dance to the sound of their own voices only, having no instruments of any kind whatever. The song was mild simple music, the cadence measured, but the figure of the dance quite wild and irregular. On one side stood all the old people of both sexes. These formed groups of 4 to 10 who danced in time, hardly stirring out of the same spot. All the young and active formed a large group on the other side, men, women and children mixed dancing, first up as far as the line of old people extended, then turning around and dancing down to

51

the same extent, each of this large group touching each other with closeness. This continued for about eight minutes, when, the song being finished, each person sat directly down on the ground in the spot he happened to be when the song was done. The Chief made a speech of about 1 or 2 minutes long. As soon as this was ended the song directly began and each person starting up fell to dancing the same figure as before.[2]

At subsequent villages he did not have to request the performance, as the people seemed to do it as a form of greeting. There was no greeting dance in traditional Plateau culture. It would therefore seem that the Indians regarded Thompson as a messenger from Chief, and when he appeared, they danced for him just as they did for other supernatural messengers.[3] Thus from village to village, prophet dances were performed in response to Thompson's visit, spurring a great awakening among the Plateau people, who began, as a result, to anticipate the imminence of Coyote's return.[4] Only one more condition remained to complete the unfolding of Chief's agenda. The Prophets had foretold that the strange messengers from the rising sun would bring a book and would teach the Indians everything. The Plateau people still needed to secure the strangers' book before the new millennium could begin.[5]

Though he was a good Christian and had set off a remarkable religious revival, neither Thompson nor his followers were in a position to provide the expected book. As commercial pioneers in a highly competitive and violent business, North West Company traders were too busy establishing new posts and ducking Blackfoot, Hudson's Bay Company, and American hostilities.[6] This did not, however, prevent the working out of the prophecy. Thompson had prepared the field and others were waiting to cultivate it.

In line with the prophecy, the Plateau Indians got their first instruction in Christian beliefs from a "different kind of man from the rising sun," but these were not white men. The first people to carry the Christian message to the Plateau were a band of Iroquois who had left the Catholic mission at Caughnawaga about 1812. About 1820 they arrived on the Plateau, where they met the grossly underpopulated Flathead. The Indians described this meeting to Father Lawrence Palladino, who reported: "Having reached the land of our Indians these Indians were kindly and hospitably received, and here the wandering band concluded to remain. The ties of friendship soon ripened into stronger ones by intermarriage, and from this on, these Iroquois became members of the Selish or Flat Head nation."[7]

The chief of this Iroquois band, Old Ignace, quickly assumed a role in Plateau prophecy. Motivated by a proselyting nature and a desire to attain recognition and leadership among his new tribe, the old Iroquois immediately undertook to instruct the Flathead in the basic elements of religion as he understood them. As described by Palladino, "Old Ignace soon acquired an ascendency and great influence over the tribe, which he wielded for the temporal and spiritual welfare of his adopted brethren. Often he would speak to them of the Catholic religion, its teachings, its prayers and its rites."[8]

This, no doubt, was very welcome to the millennium-anticipating Eastern Salish, who quickly adopted many of the rites and observances that Old Ignace showed them, applying, of course, their own significance to them. The new knowledge spread across the Plateau with the same rapidity as the prophet dance complex. In fact, Old Ignace's teachings were appended to that cult, forming a new and even more dynamic complex. The records of the early explorers and fur traders testify to the rapid spread of the new faith. There is no mention of Christian or Christian-like practices among the Plateau Indians in the journals of the Lewis and Clark Expedition or of the early fur traders; yet, by the early 1830s, morning and evening prayers, grace at meals, and the observance of the Sabbath had become so thoroughly accepted throughout the Plateau that hardly an explorer or trader failed to notice them.[9]

Since the original prophecies, the Plateau people had been led to expect not only the white people, but their religion as well. The rapid spread of the amalgamated faith was an expression of that anticipation, now rendered more urgent by the realization of the first phases of the prophecies.[10] In addition, there was a superficial similarity between the moral and structural elements of the prophet cult and Christianity, reinforcing the legitimacy of the former, the acceptability of the latter, and the potential for the confusion of the two.[11]

This composite faith was not enough, however, to satisfy the conditions set forth in the prophecy. Still needed were the white man's book and more expert instruction. Even Old Ignace was aware of that, "the conclusion of all his discourses being always the same, namely the advantage and necessity of having the Black Robes or Catholic missionaries among them by whom they could be instructed and taught the way to heaven."[12] Then, as if in perfect harmony with the words of the Prophets, developments began to take place in the fur trade that would bring both teachers and the coveted book to the people.

At the same time that Christian principles were being added to Plateau lore, the fur trade was penetrating more deeply. The merger of the North West and the Hudson's Bay companies in 1821 settled the trade conflicts that had partially paralyzed their activities. In charge of the new corporate giant's business in the area was the young, energetic, and very ambitious George Simpson. Driven by his desire to succeed in his new post, Simpson was nonetheless faced with several problems. First, American competitors were beginning to penetrate the area, threatening to rekindle the kind of conflicts the merger had just eliminated. Exacerbating that problem was the question of whether the British or the Americans owned the Plateau. Second, a shortage of furs was being created by conservation efforts in the Northern Department. Simpson responded with a policy of total exploitation of Plateau resources: an all-out effort to trap the area bare. To execute this policy he sent 220 men into the mountains in 1822, a number that was to increase continually until 1829, by which time the area was virtually denuded of fur-bearing animals.[13]

This deepened penetration made possible the kind of instruction in religious practices that the prophecy had led the Indians to expect. This is not to say that Simpson was a missionary at heart; on the contrary, his considerable correspondence contains nothing to suggest any religious, let alone evangelizing, impulses.[14] Simpson had even gone so far as to tell his colleague Andrew Colvile that educated Indians were useless both to themselves and to society. In this he was in accord with his superiors, who felt that converting Indians to European ways was acceptable only so far as it was unavoidable.[15]

Several things made attempts to educate the Indians unavoidable. First, there was a great deal of pressure from home. London's Church Missionary Society for Africa and the East brought so much pressure to bear on the Hudson's Bay Company that the firm became one of the society's principal agents. Therefore, even though business scruples militated against it, when the missionaries announced that "*Education* must be our main object in the way of preparation for Indian Evangelization," the company adopted a policy of educating Indian children. This led to the building of an Indian academy at the Red River Settlement, in the very heart of Simpson's territory.[16]

Second, and more important in motivating Simpson, was his intense drive to improve the trade on the Plateau. One of the consistent problems he had encountered was Indian apathy and independence. As one Nez Perce ethnologist has reported, "we lacked interest in fur trapping,"[17] a conclusion that Simpson confirmed in a report from Fort Nez Perce:

> This post has been progressively improving for these last three years but the profit it yields is still very moderate. . . . Its returns this season are estimated at 2000 Beaver got principally from a branch of the Nez Perces tribe called the Caiuses and it does not appear to me that there is any prospect of any considerable increase unless trappers are introduced as the Indians cannot be prevailed on to exert themselves in hunting; they are very independent of us requiring but few of our supplies and it is not until absolutely in need of an essential article of finery such as Guns & Beads that they will take the trouble of hunting.[18]

In adopting the company's and the missionary society's policy, however, Simpson believed he saw a solution to the problem:

There may be a difference of opinion as to the effect the conversion of the Indians might have on the trade; I cannot however
foresee that it could be at all injurious, on the contrary I believe it
would be highly beneficial thereto as they would in time imbibe
our manners and customs and imitate us in Dress; our Supplies
would thus become necessary to them which would increase the
consumption of European produce & manufactures and in like
measure increase & benefit our trade as they would find it requi-
site to become more industrious and to turn their attention more
seriously to the Chase in order to be enabled to provide themselves with such supplies; we should moreover be enabled to
pass through their Lands in greater safety which would lighten
the expence of transport, and supplies of Provisions would be
found at every Village and among every tribe; they might like-
wise be employed on extraordinary occasions as runners Boat-
men &c and their Services in other respects turned to profit-
able account.[19]

With this in mind, one cannot help but imagine a wry smile on
Simpson's lips when he wrote:

I do not know any part of North America where the natives could
be civilized and instructed in morality and Religion at such moderate expense and with so much facility as on the Banks of the Columbia River.... The praise worthy zeal of the Missionary Society
in the cause of Religion I think would here be soon crowned with
success; they would not only have the satisfaction of ameliorating
the condition of an immence savage population but of extending
Christianity to regions where there is not even the idea of the existence of a Supreme Being.[20]

Driven by such a compelling motivation as improving profits
while ingratiating himself with both the company and the missionary society, Simpson began promoting the cause of the Gospel with marked enthusiasm. To please the society, Simpson undertook to bring in as many Indian pupils as the mission school
at Red River could serve. As he departed on an 1825 tour of his
domain, Simpson promised the resident minister that he would
draft ten Swampy Cree, five Assiniboin, five Chipewyan, three
Carrier, and two Indian boys from the Columbia Plateau and
bring them in "as soon as practicable."[21]

Ever a man of his word, Simpson assigned Alexander Ross to the task of finding suitable candidates for the school. According to the society's representative at Red River, the Reverend David Jones, Ross reported:

> They were very indignant when he first, at the insistence of Governor Simpson, solicited their giving up their sons; and asked him if they "were looked upon as dogs—willing to give up their children to go they knew not whither": but when he told them that they were going to a Minister of Religion to learn how to know and serve God, they said he might have *"Hundreds of children in an hour's time."*[22]

Ross declined that offer, selecting only two boys. One was reportedly the son of the Spokan chief and was given the name Garry, after Company factor Nicholas Garry. The other was initially alleged to be the son of a Flathead chief, but it was later discovered that he was actually a Kutenai. He was given the name Pelly, after Hudson's Bay Governor J. H. Pelly.[23]

Both Kutenai Pelly and Spokan Garry were avid students and quick learners. Within two years they had learned enough about the white man's religion to meet rather stringent qualifications for baptism. The Reverend Mr. Jones himself performed the ceremony on 27 June 1827.[24] Within another two years they had made sufficient progress that the authorities decided the boys could be sent home for a visit,[25] but the trip was to be more than a vacation. One very necessary object was to reacquaint the two young men with their native languages, which the explorer David Douglas claims that they had forgotten.[26] They were also charged with the task of bringing in more students for the Red River School. In accomplishing that task, they were to get their first taste of preaching, an internship of sorts before they completed their studies.[27] They were, therefore, entrusted with the sacred task of being the first people to bring the white man's book to the Plateau.

Upon their return, their people hailed the two young men as great prophets, and their arrival spurred another Plateau-wide revival.[28] This spread the Christianized prophet dance to corners of the Plateau where it had not been practiced before and reinforced its strength everywhere else.[29] But there was no way to harness this explosive energy. Pelly and Garry were only two men with two Bibles, and although they traveled widely, they could not spread the white man's knowledge far enough—they could not teach the Indians "everything." All they could do was take five more chiefs' sons to be trained as teachers and hope that their mentor, the Reverend Jones, could send white missionaries to complete the work.[30]

Unfortunately, owing to a series of developments in England, the Church Missionary Society found itself financially embarrassed. It was forced to abandon a number of its plans, including one to send laborers into the Pacific Northwest. So, when the boys returned to the Red River Settlement in the spring of 1831, they left behind the kind of turmoil that would announce the nearing millennium, but no instruments for carrying it to its conclusion.[31] Yet, as I have said, prophecies have a peculiar way of working themselves out. Just when it appeared that the millennium was to be indefinitely deferred, the conjoined forces of mammon and Zion were pushing the unfolding process toward completion.

In the fall of 1823, trappers employed by William Ashley had stumbled across the South Pass. The ease with which this pass could be traveled, coupled with Indian hostilities and depleted beaver populations in the Missouri region, prompted Ashley to shift his operations to the west side of the Rockies, a move that added greatly to his profits. According to Hiram Chittenden, Ashley's average take of $61,500 per year made quite an impression on his competitors.[32] Such unprecedented success led all of the companies then based in St. Louis to begin looking westward. Centering around an annual rendezvous point, their agents set up a trade network that spanned the entire northern Rockies. In the process, they established relations with a number of tribes that previously had been tied to the Hudson's Bay Company or totally unconnected with the fur trade, among these, the Flathead and Nez Perce. Here the Americans were in a position to play their role in the unfolding prophetic agenda.[33]

Just as the trappers were putting their plans into effect, a Nez

Perce named Hol-lol-sote-tote was playing his role in guaranteeing the success of the prophecy. Hol-lol-sote-tote was a chief's son, intelligent, and a very talented linguist. These qualities led to his being sent in the winter of 1830 to hear Spokan Garry and to bring the message from the white man's God back to his people. Like many similar messengers, he carried back both the words and the excitement, spurring a religious revival among the Nez Perce.[34] Nez Perce traditions report that his message was the primary subject of conversation around their fires all during the winter of 1830. The Nez Perce also carried the message to the Flathead, who then joined them in their deliberations.[35]

These deliberations centered around two basic issues. First, even though two of the boys who accompanied Pelly and Garry back to Red River were Nez Perce, the actions of the Church Missionary Society must have seemed agonizingly slow to people who were looking forward to the end of the world. Second, the British missionaries were tied to the Hudson's Bay Company, with whom the Nez Perce had little patience.[36]

The solution may well have been posed by Hol-lol-sote-tote himself, for he was the son of Walammotinin, the man who had hosted Lewis and Clark. Remembering the extravagant promises that the Americans had made and aware that the American fur traders were underselling their British competitors, it may have occurred to this young man that an arrangement with the Americans might be possible. In any case, the Indians decided that a joint Nez Perce-Flathead party would venture out in the spring of 1831 to find the American traders in the mountains. Then they would find out what the Americans could do about supplying guns, missionaries, or both.[37]

This Indian expedition met the fur traders in the mountains of Montana on 30 May 1831. Trapper Warren Angus Ferris, who left a record of this meeting, does not reveal what transpired between his companions and the Flathead-Nez Perce party beyond mention of some strategic discussions concerning Blackfoot raiding parties thought to be in the area.[38] Therefore it is impossible to learn from this account whose idea it was for a small committee of Indians to accompany one detachment of Americans to the annual trade rendezvous or how the Indian delegation got from the rendezvous to St. Louis. While he was exploring the Rocky Mountains in 1835, future Oregon missionary Marcus Whitman tried to learn the truth behind the story that had sent him more than two thousand miles into the wilderness. He noted the results of his investigation in his journal:

> The following is the history of those Indians that came to St. Louis to gain knowledge of the Christian religion, as I received it from the trader (Fontenelle), under whose protection they came and returned. He says their object was to gain religious knowledge. For this purpose the Flathead tribe delegated one of their principal chiefs and two of their principal men, and the Napiersa [Nez Perce] tribe a like delegation, it being a joint delegation of both tribes. In addition to this delegation a young napiersa came along. When they came to Council Bluff, two of the Flatheads and one of the Napiersa returned home, and the other Flathead, the chief and the Napiersa chief, and the remaining one of the delegation and the young Indian came to St. Louis, where they remained through the winter.[39]

Normally, this delegation would simply have blended in with the countless bands of Indians and fur traders that moved into and out of St. Louis during the heyday of the Rocky Mountain fur trade. The dynamic force of manifesting prophecy, however, made this situation anything but normal. It is still a total mystery how it all came to pass, but the circumstances surrounding the Flathead-Nez Perce delegation were instantly mythologized. The resulting myth became both a lasting part of Western folklore and the pivotal factor in the coming together of the white and Indian prophets.

According to the myth, another Indian delegation was, by coincidence, in St. Louis at the same time that the Flathead-Nez Perce delegation was there. This other delegation consisted of several Wyandot leaders, including a white adoptee named William Walker. Upon arriving in St. Louis, Walker stopped to visit William Clark, who was then superintendent of Indian affairs in the Far West. During the visit the superintendent reportedly mentioned that he was presently hosting three chiefs of the Flathead nation.[40] The story continues that Walker was overcome by curiosity and stepped into an adjoining room, where he claims to have seen the visitors:

> I was struck with their appearance. They differ in appearance from any tribe of Indians I have ever seen: small in size, delicately formed, small limbs, and the most exact symmetry throughout, except the head. I had always supposed from their being called "Flatheads," that the head was actually flat on top; but this is not the case. The head is flattened thus:
> From the point of the nose to the apex of the head, there is a perfect straight line, the protuberance of the forehead is flattened or leveled.[41]

In true mythic style, the strangers' grotesque appearance contrasted sharply with their noble purpose. According to the myth:

> It appeared that some white man had penetrated into their country, and happened to be a spectator at one of their religious ceremonies, which they scrupulously performed at stated periods. He informed them that their mode of worshipping the supreme Being was radically wrong, and instead of being acceptable and pleasing, it was displeasing to him; he also informed them that the white people *away* toward the rising of the sun had been put in possession of the true mode of worshipping the great Spirit. They had a book containing directions how to conduct themselves in order to enjoy his favor and hold converse with him; and with this guide, no one need go astray; but every one that would follow the directions laid down there could enjoy, in this life, his favor, and after death would be received into the country where the great Spirit resides, and live for ever with him.[42]

They had thus come to St. Louis seeking the true mode of worship that only the white people possessed.

All myths contain many levels of truth, and this one is no exception. The account of Walker's meeting with the Rocky Mountain Indians is probably totally false, as is the account it contains of their discovery of the white man's mode of worship.[43] Still, the essence of the myth is truthful. In a far less fanciful report than Walker's, Joseph Rosati, the Catholic bishop of St. Louis, stated that two of his priests visited the delegation and reported that the Indians had made the sign of the cross and apparently had requested baptism. According to the bishop, such things had been taught them by two Indians who had been to Canada, where they had witnessed the "beautiful ceremonies of the Catholic faith."[44] Thus regardless of the veracity of any given version of the story, it was apparent that the Flathead and Nez Perce who ventered to St. Louis had done so in search of God, but neither Walker nor Rosati could have known just how different the Indians' conception was from their own. Instead, both put out the call that God, as they conceived of Him, had prepared the Indians for deliverance from their benighted state.[45]

In the United States, the Walker myth came to the knowledge of a pious businessman named G. P. Disoway, who passed it on to the Methodist-operated *Christian Advocate and Journal and Zion's Herald* for publication. In his cover letter, which was published with Walker's report, Disoway played the mythic quality of the delegation story to the hilt. First calling attention to the way that the Indians supposedly defaced the divine image through their grotesque head-flattening practices, Disoway goes on to paint an affecting portrait of savages motivated by the providence of God to seek enlightenment. He then calls for action: "Let the Church awake from her slumbers and go forth in her strength to the salvation of these wandering sons of our native forests."[46]

This appeal reached an audience well attuned to the message. Like the Plateau Indians, Protestant Americans, too, had been listening to prophets and waiting for the beginning of a millennial process. By coincidence or design, the Plateau delegation fitted perfectly. Thus a coincidence led to a myth, and that, in turn, led to a misunderstanding that brought two very different prophetic traditions together.

CHAPTER 5

The White Prophecy

In 1836 social and political commentator Calvin Colton observed of the decades since the American Revolution: "We have watched the peculiar, uneasy and susceptible character of the age, and observed the powerful and irresistible tendencies to change throughout the civilized world, in politics, morals, and religion. The popular mass have discovered and felt things are not right, and have been easily moved to favour any enterprise that promised to make them better."[1] Though historians have disagreed over the true nature of this period, few have questioned Colton's assertion about its restlessness. The "tendencies to change" must, indeed, have seemed "irresistible."

Geographical expansion was one form of change that was both gross and widely influential. In 1800 the entire area of land under the jurisdiction of the United States was 864,746 square miles. By 1820 this had increased by over 100 percent, and by 1850 the total was up to 2,940,042 square miles. More significantly, human geography followed suit. For example, Ohio's population grew from 45,000 in 1800 to 231,000 in 1810 and continued to grow at an average rate of more than 75 percent per decade over the next forty years. With a national growth rate of only 34 percent, Ohio's population explosion indicates both an intense interest in the West and the beginnings of a major demographic shift.[2]

The westward movement was made possible by a proportional revolution in the means of transportation. In the antebellum period, communication networks developed based on three great innovations: steamboats, canals, and steam railroads. These allowed manufactured necessities and consumer goods to flow over the Alleghenies and up the Mississippi; they also made it possible to ship farm produce, lumber, and other western products to the world market at a competitive price. It has been estimated that in the 1820s the steamboat lowered downstream shipping rates by 70–75 percent and upstream rates by as much as 95 percent. This commerce promoted the rapid development of the trans-Appalachian frontier more than any other cause.[3]

Some idea of how comprehensive the effects of these innovations were is suggested by the amount of money spent in making them. Between 1800 and 1836 federal aid for internal improvements increased consistently. For example, the $702,000 that the John Quincy Adams administration spent annually for such projects was nearly doubled by the Jacksonians who followed them in office. These figures, however, are dwarfed by the amount that the individual states invested. During the years 1835–1837, for instance, the states incurred a combined debt of over $60,000,000 from canal building alone, a figure roughly equivalent to $360,000,000 in 1970 currency.[4]

That such investments were made reflect great confidence, not only in the developmental potential of the West, but in the growth potential of the national economy as well. Such confidence was not misplaced. Between 1790 and 1840, Americans witnessed unparalleled economic growth that, with some interruptions, allowed an increase in both national and individual prosperity throughout the era. For example, the value of American exports increased from $20.2 million in 1790 to $108.3 million in 1807, and the net earnings from carrying those exports increased even more dramatically. Although America's involvement in foreign wars interrupted this dynamic prosperity between 1808 and 1814, in the next two decades, not only did the national economy grow, but the consumer enjoyed very substantial improvements in real income.[5]

In reaction to these political, economic, and intellectual forces, Americans found themselves forming a political and social system with some similarities to that on the Plateau. Like their Indian counterparts, antebellum Americans voiced an ideological commitment to liberty and equality. At the same time, American political figures recognized that there were natural spiritual and physical differences between people, and like the Plateau Indians, they sought a political form that would permit this "natural aristocracy" to rise to the top. As expressed by Thomas Jefferson: "May we not even say, that that form of government is the best, which provides the most effectually for a pure selection of these natural aristoi into the offices of government?"[6] This realization led thinkers like Jefferson to conclude that "the influence over government must be shared among all the people. . . . It has been thought that corruption is restrained by confining the right of suffrage to a few of the wealthier of the people: but it would be more effectually restrained by an extension of that right to such numbers as would bid defiance to the means of corruption."[7]

Offered such an invitation, Americans turned to public affairs with enthusiasm. Anxious to remove artificial barriers to their individual destinies, they sought to prevent entrenchment. Since the founding of the Republic there had been a grass-roots movement to equalize suffrage rights. Emphasizing the removal of property ownership as a prerequisite for voting, this movement had been gathering momentum for thirty years by the beginning of the 1820s; in that decade most barriers set against it were removed. By 1830, eighteen states had liberalized their voting laws, a trend that was to continue until 1850, when only North Carolina maintained the elitist policy that Jefferson had argued against.[8]

In religion, as in the social and political arenas, common men refused to accept artificial barriers. Beginning at the turn of the century, a religious movement to match the tumultuous times swept through America, earning the name the Second Great Awakening. Firing the religious emotions of the common man, the awakening's steady burning was never extinguished from its lighting at Cane River, Kentucky in 1801 until it was finally smothered by the Civil War.[9] Analysts have described the awakening's theology as essentially Arminian. Disdaining the Calvinistic belief in predestination, radical theologians like Charles G. Finny adopted the ideas of Nathaniel W. Taylor. Taylorism taught that man is responsible for his own sin and that salvation is freely offered to all. Those who choose to accept God's grace will be saved, and only those who reject God will suffer for the sin of Adam.[10]

In the village church or at the neighborhood camp meeting, the theology was often reduced to a few simple maxims that even the least intellectually inclined parishioners could comprehend. What the theology was called made very little difference to such listeners as long as what they heard was consistent with what they knew, and this new religious philosophy accorded well with their needs.[11] The awakening succeeded because the preachers gave the masses the sort of religion they wanted. In the process, religion was made something familiar, something that accorded with everyday experience, and therefore, something that helped the common man to make sense of his ever more complex world.[12]

Another, and perhaps more significant accomplishment of the Second Great Awakening was to give common men something in common. The broad spectrum covered by the theology and its openness to interpretation created a synthesis so far-reaching that most Americans could identify with it. They may have argued the fine points of doctrine, but they agreed on the field of debate. This shared religious persuasion gave Americans a common ground upon which a national identity could be forged from the many disparate factions that had come together to create the Republic. So, like their Plateau contemporaries, white Americans found a religious validation for their confederacy.[13]

In this process, the aims and methods of evangelical Protestantism and democratic liberalism became inseparably linked. One evangelical organization, the American Home Missionary Society, went so far as to proclaim in its constitution that it was "doing a work of patriotism, no less than that of Christianity." The document then went on to point out that the unification of missionary efforts was "indispensable to the moral advancement and the political stability of the United States."[14] The syncretic linkage helped to create an even more evangelical attitude. Central to the persuasion was the concept of millennialism. To reborn American Protestants there was no question that God had a plan for the universe, and it was an article of faith that there would be a thousand-year peace under the reign of Christ before the plan reached its end. Many were so carried away by this concept that they began to expect the millennium to begin at any instant and therefore abandoned all mundane occupations to wait for the coming glory. Others were more patient, but no less adamant.[15] What both sorts had in common was an abiding faith that America occupied a special place in God's plan and that the seat of Christ's government would be here. As voiced by one of the leading evangelicals during the height of the Second Great Awakening, "It was the opinion of [Jonathan] Edwards that the millennium would commence in America. When I first encountered this opinion, I thought it Chimerical: but all providential signs of the times, lend corroboration to it."[16]

The attainment of this paradise was not to come without some effort. Central to the millenarian script was the concept of Armageddon, the great confrontation between the forces of good and evil. If America was to be the site of the millennium, then America would also be the site of this confrontation and as the champion for God's side, America would be the primary target for the forces of evil. It is not surprising that the nation conceived of itself as being surrounded by enemies. The Old World, especially the Catholic countries, were considered the primary seat of evil. Thomas Hart Benton spoke for many when he said, "The European Legitimates hold everything American in contempt and detestation" and warned his fellow countrymen to be on their guard.[17] The country was, however, in an enviable position where national security was concerned. Separated from Europe by thousands of miles of ocean, Americans had little to fear from invading Old World armies. Furthermore, as the Reverend Alexander McLeod sermonized at the close of the War of 1812, "The veterans of Wellington attest the prowess of our troops; and the world is astonished at the facility with which our naval heroes have conquered, when they met upon terms of equality, those who have conquered all other nations."[18]

The primary threat, then, was infiltration and subversion, the very type of war the corrupt and treacherous Europeans of the American imagination would wage. Of course such nativistic paranoia was nothing new to Americans, but it grew most virulent during this era. Otherwise responsible and intelligent men began to interpret unrelated events as evidence of a worldwide conspiracy against American liberties.[19]

A leading proponent of this conspiracy theory was Samuel F. B. Morse. In a series of articles, Morse pointed out that, having reestablished despotic tyranny after the defeat of Napoleonic liberalism, the Holy Alliance found "the silent but powerful and increasing influence of our institutions" threatening to their rule. According to Morse, the influence of Friedrich von Schlegel's philosophy and Prince Metternich's political machinations had prompted Austria to sponsor a secret organization called the Leopold Society and to fill its ranks with Jesuits, whom the Austrian government gifted with one hundred thousand dollars to cover expenses. Through this organization, Morse insisted, Metternich sought "to send Popery to this country if it is not here, or give it a fresh and vigorous impulse if it is already here. . . . She has set herself to work with all her activity, to disseminate throughout the country the Popish religion."[20] The objective was to undermine the American way of life. To Morse and his fellows firebrands, Catholicism was the natural ally of authoritarianism and was, therefore, "opposed in its whole character to Republican liberty." As the "promoter and supplier of arbitrary power," the Catholic church would insinuate itself into American life, destroy the great democratic experiment, and in the process, eliminate God's gathering host.[21]

Of course the presence of the Catholic church would not have deflected true American Protestants from the proper course, but according to Protestant activists, the devious Europeans had worked out a solution to that problem. If the current population was impervious to the influence of the priests, these authoritarian plotters would simply alter the population. This aspect of the conspiracy was vividly explained by Morse's fellow incendiary, Lyman Beecher:

> If the potentates of Europe have no designs upon our liberties, what means the paying of the passage and emptying out upon our shores such floods of pauper emigrants—the contents of the poor house and the sweepings of the streets?—multiplying tumults and violence, filling our prisons, and crowding our workhouses, and quadrupling our taxation, and sending annually accumulating thousands to the polls to lay their inexperienced hand upon the helm of our power?[22]

It was not, however, the newcomers' inexperience or their tumultuousness that Beecher feared most. As he went on to say,

> it should appear that three-fourths of the foreign emigrants whose accumulating tide is rolling in upon us, are, through the medium of their religion and priesthood, as entirely accessible to the control of the potentates of Europe as if they were an army of soldiers, enlisted and officered, and spreading over the land.[23]

In this way, the forces of evil would be brought up to full fighting strength and would be completely prepared when the trumpets sounded announcing Armageddon. Worse yet, there was the possibility that the evil ones might be able to undermine God's plan for the universe by polluting America before the millennium could begin.

Many Americans believed that the frontier was the area most vulnerable to infiltration. As early as the 1770s, there was sentiment that the United States could not be secure while Old World powers had possessions in North America, and this sentiment did not fade.[24] Millennialists continually stressed that demonic foreign powers might seduce and then combine forces with the "wild and disaffected" Indians on the frontier to launch an offensive that would devastate the country. In 1824 the quartermaster general warned Congress of this possibility, pointing out that such a combination would be "more formidable to us than any force which Europe combined could oppose to us."[25] Secretary of War John Calhoun repeated the warning in 1829 and was backed up by expert testimony from such authorities as fur traders Joshua Pilcher, Jedediah Smith, David Jackson, and William Sublette.[26] Even though, as one letter put it, "the injury which must happen to the United States is too obvious to need a recapitulation," concerned Americans like Senator Lewis Linn continued to recapitulate for another decade.[27]

Though the problems of infiltration and frontier conflict were serious, many Americans put their faith in God and awaited a divine inspiration. The faithful were rewarded with a solution that not only put their fears to rest but actually helped them to prepare the world for the coming of the millennium. The first stage in this solution lay in arming the nation against the forces of evil. "And what are the weapons of this warfare?" Morse asked in an 1835 pamphlet.

> The Bible, the Tract, the Infant school, the Sunday school, the common school for all classes, the college and university for all classes, a free press for the discussion of all questions. These, all these, are weapons of Protestantism, weapons unknown to Popery.
>
> We must make *an immediate, a vigorous, a united, a persevering effort to spread religious and intellectual cultivation through every part of our country.*[28]

Thus was the nation to be converted so that it could present a united front to the evil world. At the same time, God's work of saving the unfaithful would be carried out, thereby advancing His unfolding plan for the universe. Also in the process, America would prove it was deserving of being God's chosen nation.

The second stage lay in seizing control of the frontier before evil Europeans could grasp it and turn the savage occupants against America. This meant expanding not only American authority over the wilderness but American institutions and culture as well. The Protestant awakening and its syncretism with American liberalism prepared Americans well for this task. A distinguishing characteristic of the resulting reborn culture was a belief in its own superiority, accompanied by the altruistic conviction that it should be shared by all people. This self-assured selflessness prompted reborn Americans to become as evangelical about their culture as they were about their religion.[29]

The combined need to control the frontier and to convert the unconverted endowed American expansionism with a very special character: America was to expand, not for its own aggrandizement, but to fulfill its preordained role in God's eternal plan. The object for the evangelicals was to be nothing less than moral reform of the world, which would entail remodeling it in America's image.[30] This mission found full expression in the movement to annex what was then called the "Oregon Country." As early as 1820, congressional expansionists had been urging the take-over of the Far West for national security. In 1821 and again in 1822, Representative John Floyd of Virginia had proposed that federal land grants be given to any American citizen who would settle in Oregon, that a naval fortress and customs house be built at the mouth of the Columbia River, and that an Indian office be established and vested with absolute control of all intercultural intercourse.[31] On both occasions, the Oregon bill was killed by the argument that expansion would drain the United States of wealth and population, thereby irreparably weakening both government and nation. Furthermore, unregenerated congressmen like Silas Wood and Albert Tracy believed such expansion would make the United States a colonial power in violation of its national principles. They warned that the western colonies would rebel eventually, creating an additional threat to national security.[32]

By 1825, however, enough congressmen had been "born again" that the enlightening of the world took its place alongside national security to form a new and more powerful colonial cant. In that year, Benton told Congress that the implantation of American institutions on the Pacific coast would confer "great and wonderful benefits" upon the Chinese and Japanese; that "science, liberal principles in government, and true religion, might cast their lights across the intervening sea." Through this process, the "inhabitants of the oldest and the newest, the most despotic and the freest Governments, would become the neighbors, and, peradventure, the friends of each other."[33] In this way, American institutions would be expanded abroad, strengthened at home, and defended from hostile forces by the shared interests of East Asia and North America.

This world-saving argument was developed even further by Hall Jackson Kelley. Between 1828 and 1832 Kelley wrote numerous letters to congressmen and government officials outlining the value of Oregon to the nation. His primary justification was the extension, improvement, and protection of free government, which in Oregon would be "founded on equality of justice, and the rights of man."[34] The results would stand as a "stupendous column, resting on the best materials of earth—extending into the heavens, and sustaining the moral world." The benefits of the enterprise would eventually "cover the earth as the waters cover the sea. Then will the peaceful generations look back upon our times with a painful remembrance of the half-civilized character of their forefathers."[35]

Though these arguments were presented to congressional expansionists, it was Congregational expansionists who took on the challenge. Consumed with the moral self-assurance born of the awakening, ministers and would-be ministers took the lead in the Oregon expansion movement, lending it a special evangelical stamp. As early as 1822 S. Adams, a student at Andover Seminary, had conducted extensive research on the practicability of missions in the Pacific Northwest.[36] Adams reported to the Society of Inquiry Respecting Missions that the Indians in the area possessed "noble traits of mind" indicating to the reporter that if the savages could be "brought under the influence of good education and the Christian religion, they would be as good materials as the church ever had to help her cause." He concluded by saying that the church had to aid in stopping the "exterminating process" and become involved in raising "the oppressed Indian to the comforts and happiness of civilized life, and set down with him hereafter with Abraham and Isaac, and Jacob in the Kingdom of God."[37]

Though this mission was their primary motivation, Christian associations heeded and paid homage to Manifest Destiny as well. In its annual report for the year 1827, the American Board of Commissioners for Foreign Missions (ABCFM) noted: "The tide of emigration is rolling westward so rapidly, that it must speedily surmount every barrier, till it reaches every habitable part of this continent."[38] Unable to halt such an overwhelming force, the commissioners resolved that they should promote emigration and settlement in order, perhaps, to control it, as their 1827 report so clearly stated:

> the first mission which shall be fitted out for this region will be accompanied by a little colony; which, though distinct in its organization, and in some sense secular as to its object, will be formed and sent forth with the same views, and for the accomplishment of the same great end. . . . In this manner, early provision will be made for the religious wants of the adventurous voyager and the fearless man of the woods, who shall meet in these remote regions.[39]

The ABCFM's Prudential Committee, acting promptly on this manifesto, instructed their establishment in the Sandwich Islands to explore the issue further. Within two years an agent named J. S. Green secured passage on a vessel and sailed from the islands toward the Oregon coast to determine whether a missionary colony could be planted there and if so, where the best location would be. He arrived on the Northwest Coast in March 1829 and sailed up and down the shore for the next six months, putting in wherever possible. He discovered that the presence of white traders had polluted the coastal Indians to the point that saving them would require a much more massive effort than the missionary societies had supposed. He went on to suggest, however, that the areas around the Columbia and Umpqua rivers might prove suitable.[40]

Weighing all the considerations, the Hawaiian Standing Committee on Oregon Missions decided that "the indications of providence in regard to the immediate establishment of a mission on the North West Coast, are not sufficiently plain to warrant this Mission in taking any direct step in reference to this subject." They then referred the issue back to the Prudential Committee in Boston.[41]

Providence, however, was not stalled. While Green had been sailing around in the Pacific, the idea of Christian colonization had taken hold among humanitarian organizations, and other missionary societies soon became involved in the Oregon mission business. On 27 June 1832 the Committee on Missions of the General Conference of the Methodist Episcopal Church drafted a resolution calling for the establishment of "aboriginal missions on our western and north western frontiers" with "all practicable dispatch." The statement went on to demand that some trustworthy person or persons be appointed to explore the region and to "promptly notify the bishop nearest in his neighborhood, and also the managers of our missionary society, of the state of the Indian tribes generally, together with the prospects of introducing the Gospel among them."[42]

The call was picked up in the following month by the *Methodist Magazine and Quarterly Review*, which published a review of fur-trader Ross Cox's *Adventures on the Columbia River*.[43] The review clearly and forcefully set forth the humanitarian duty of Christian Americans: "God has given us these people as a part of our inheritance. He has given us his Gospel and commanded us to carry it to them; and the manifest tokens of his sanction on the efforts we have already made for their conversion, afford us sure earnest of future success, provided we prosecute our plans and labors in his name with vigor and perseverance."[44]

In the same month, Kelley's literary talents were pressed into service; the *American Traveller* printed one of Kelley's many letters. In it, Kelley lamented, "From the influence of causes in my own bosom, I have long found it impossible to contemplate the deplorable condition of the Aborigines of this Continent, and not wish to benefit them with the improved and increased blessings which it is the felicity of an enlightened and virtuous people to enjoy."[45] He expressed the millenarian significance of this mission more clearly than most: "When christendom shall have passed into Oregon and other heathen and dark regions, her best population, carrying with them the ever-burning lights of the gospel; then will mankind realize something like the halcyon era of universal peace."[46]

All that remained was to extend the new American faith into the wilderness. Therein lay the final and most perfect justification for American expansionism: a holy commandment pushing the faithful into the recognition that the unfolding of divine providence could come only through American expansion. In the process, the Indians would be saved and their salvation would provide both the symbol of and the key to the American millennium.

CHAPTER 6

The Prophets Meet

News of the Nez Perce and Flathead delegation hit the national press only months after the publication of Kelley's millenarian pronouncement. The "peculiar, uneasy, and susceptible character of the age" had primed the people for a westward explosion of Protestant American beliefs and institutions. In seeking their own revelations, the Plateau people provided the triggering device that would propel the Americans toward them, bringing closer the realization of both Indian and white prophecies.

The Methodists were the first among the reborn Americans to respond to the Indians' request for aid. On 20 March 1833 the Methodist Missionary Board directed its corresponding secretary to inquire into the feasibility and propriety of establishing a mission among the Flathead and Nez Perce.[1] While this investigation proceeded in official circles, church members made it abundantly clear that they had no reservations about the propriety of such an establishment. Throughout April 1833 people wrote to the *Christian Advocate* offering advice, encouragement, and contributions of both money and services to help establish a Flathead mission. Motivated by the belief that the unfolding of Christian providence had been revealed in the coming of the Flathead delegation, reborn Americans insisted that duty required an immediate response. One correspondent, A. M'Allister, stated the case with particular flair:

> How ominous this visit of the Cho-pun-nish and Flat Head Indians! How loud the call to the missionary spirit of the age! It calls to my mind a declaration made by Bishop Soule, when preaching at a camp in this country. Speaking of the missionary zeal of the Methodist preachers, of their extended field of labors, their untiring perseverance to compass the earth and spread Scriptural holiness through all the world: "We will not cease," said he, "until we shall have planted the standard of Christianity high on the summit of the Stony Mountains."
>
> Already would it seem that a door is open, and the Indians from the lofty summit of the Rocky Mountains look far east with burning desire to behold the coming of the messenger of God.[2]

The Methodists quickly displayed the "untiring perseverance" to which M'Allister had alluded. On the very day he wrote his note, the Mission Board reported favorably on the subject of a Flathead mission. Three months later they made Jason Lee the official missionary to the Flathead. The planned mission was to be of the same general type outlined by the ABCFM back in 1827. Lee was to be the superintendent, and his nephew Daniel was appointed second missionary. They were to find colonists to join them from among "persons in the Western Country who from their proximity to the Indian Country had become somewhat acquainted with the Indian character and manner of life." Once assembled, this little company was to venture into the wilderness, set up shop, and then send for reinforcements if the situation warranted.[3] The Lees were completely successful in establishing a Christian colony in Oregon, but it was nowhere near the Flathead or Nez Perce. Two weeks after the party arrived at Fort Vancouver in September 1834, Lee gave up the idea of establishing a mission in the mountains. He chose, instead, to locate the establishment fifty miles up the Willamette River from the Hudson's Bay Company Fort.[4]

Though Lee had failed, the twin forces of the Plateau prophecy and the Christian revelation went on pushing events forward. On 10 April 1832 the ABCFM had received a letter from a Reverend Samuel Parker demanding that they become involved in the Oregon mission. Reacting to the Flathead delegation, Parker had told the board that "the whole world evidently presents a field white for the harvest." He went on to criticize the board for their past slowness, saying that "the heathen themselves are chiding Christians for their negligence in not obeying the commandment 'go ye into all of the world, and preach the gospel to every creature.'" Ever since reading about the "Wise Men of the West," he continued, he had asked himself "Am I doing my duty to those who are perishing without the gospel?" Resolving that he was not, Parker volunteered to establish a mission among the "Flat-head Indians, or some other tribe."[5]

After nearly two years of debate over the cost of the enterprise, Parker's qualifications, and the propriety of entering into a field thought to be under Methodist cultivation, the board finally approved an exploring tour to the Rocky Mountains. Unfortunately, Parker and the two associates the board had assigned to him got to St. Louis too late in the spring of 1834 to tie up with the caravan of the American Fur Company. Without expert guides, there was no way for the party to proceed. After a brief stay in St. Louis, Parker finally went home.[6]

Imbued with the spirit of the Second Great Awakening, however, Parker was not ready to give up. Immediately on returning to the East, he began lobbying for another chance to explore the mountains for a mission site.[7] His persistence was rewarded by the news, on 7 January 1835, that he and one assistant were to venture to the Rockies in the following spring. A week later he learned that his associate was to be a pious young physician named Marcus Whitman.[8]

Having learned from his previous experience, Parker got his second party to St. Louis in plenty of time to join the fur caravan departing for the mountains on 15 May 1835.[9] They continued on with the fur traders until the early fall, when they arrived at the annual rendezvous. Here, they finally encountered some Flathead and Nez Perce Indians.[10] According to both Parker's and Whitman's accounts, the Indians were very happy to see them and asked them to come to their villages immediately. The missionaries were so overwhelmed by the Indians' apparent sincerity that Whitman resolved to return to the East immediately to try to convince the ABCFM of the need for rapid action and to enlist a party of associates. He hoped that through prompt action he could return with reinforcements within a year. In the meantime, Parker was to proceed on, scout out the territory, and open the way for the coming mission.[11]

Whitman returned safely to Boston and submitted his report on 7 November 1835. In it he stated that the Indians had said that "they have always been unhappy since they have become informed of the religion of the whites they do not understand it. It has only reached their ears they wish it to affect their most vital parts." Furthermore, "they are very much inclined to follow any advice given them by the whites and are ready to adopt any thing that is taught them as religion." For this reason, Whitman stressed, it was important that no time be wasted lest they be led astray by Catholics or worse.[12]

The board agreed, approving the projected mission on 6 January 1836. All that remained, they told Whitman, was the selection of suitable companions, a process that had already begun.[13] Within a month and a half of Whitman's initial appointment, a young woman named Narcissa Prentiss had applied for the privilege "to labour for the conversion of the heathen."[14] In a letter of recommendation the Reverend O. S. Powell told the board that Prentiss was romantically involved, and he thought would eventually marry Marcus Whitman.[15] Having reviewed her qualifications and finding her acceptable, the board made Marcus and Narcissa missionary companions. The couple followed up on this action by marrying on 18 February 1836.[16]

Though interest in the mission seemed strong, the board had difficulty finding other people who could meet its rigid qualifications to accompany the Whitmans. On 6 January 1836 Whitman wrote to recommend Henry Harmon Spalding, a priggishly devout Presbyterian and ex-student of anti-Catholic firebrand Lyman Beecher. Spalding had previously applied to the board in August 1835 for a position among the Osage.[17] At that time he had been married for two years to a woman he claimed to have wed "for the express purpose of giving [her] the opportunity of pursuing the same theological studies with myself." Such magnanimity had been rewarded, Spalding had told the board, for in Eliza, "God has given me a companion that knows how to 'spin' even in those ways in my opinion well calculated for the work we presume to contemplate."[18] The board apparently had agreed, inasmuch as they granted the couple the appointment they had sought.

Whitman knew of Spalding's previous appointment, but he told the board that Spalding had agreed to accompany him instead if the board was willing to change his assignment.[19] The board communicated to Whitman their hesitance to assign the Spaldings to such a pioneer post because of possible danger to their child, and besides, they were considering the appointment of a highly recommended man named Mr. Clark. Whitman promptly responded that the Spaldings had no children, "having lost their child to death some time since."[20]

By 15 February Whitman had become desperate. In a letter to the board's corresponding secretary, David Greene, he lamented:

> In your last you say Mr Clark declines going out to the Nez-perces. I saw Mr Spaulding on his way to the Osages. He consented to accompany me if the Board saw fit to alter his designation. He had gone on and will await my arrival at Cincinnati or else your decision on the subject. I am willing to accompany Mr Spaulding as an associate yet I know little of his particular adaptiveness to that station. Perhaps no one can be more important in regard to our intercourse with the Indians. We shall have to be under the influence of both British and American traders.
> Mr Eddy does not find any willing to go.[21]

With that, the doctor sped off in pursuit, catching the Spaldings at Jamestown, New York on the seventeenth. Spalding reported that Whitman

> immediately communicated his object. It was to persuade me to alter my destiny to the Rocky Mountains. He said the objection that lay in your mind to my going to the Mountains was the idea

that we had a child. We have no child as he has already stated. He says this removed & you are perfectly willing the destiny should be changed. He said all other attempts to obtain a clergyman have failed, & that if I refused, the mission to the Rocky Mountains must be abandoned, at least for the present. Everything considered, though I had left my friends & made arrangements to go to Boudinot, I felt it my duty to consent to his request & did so I hope in the fear of God.[22]

Presented with a fait accompli, the board could do little but approve. Even so, the Whitmans departed from Rushville, New York on 3 March without knowing for sure whether they were to have the Spaldings as companions or not.[23] It was not until 9 March that the corresponding secretary wrote Whitman that the board had acted favorably on his proposal. The same letter contained word that they were to have "a Mr. Gray, a good teacher, cabinet maker and house-joiner from Utica," as the fifth member of their party. Gray, it would seem, had been discovered by Mr. Eddy on the same day that Whitman had despaired of Eddy's attempts to locate willing workers. Two days later Gray had written to the board applying specifically "to accompany Doct. Whitman to his station beyond the Rocky Mountains," and the now desperate board could hardly refuse. They appointed Gray immediately without any serious investigation into his character or suitability and sent him rushing to catch up with the already departed party.[24]

The full expedition finally came together at St. Louis in the second week of March 1836. From there, Gray and Spalding were to drive the wagons and the stock that they had acquired overland to Liberty while Whitman and the women took the baggage on the American Fur Company's steamboat. Owing to an accident on the river, however, Whitman and his wards were unable to secure passage to Liberty when the boat finally arrived on 23 March. Since the overland party had already departed, they were forced to hire a team and take off in pursuit.[25] This was just a taste of what the rest of the trip would be like, but despite delays, accidents, and quarrels, the missionaries' devotion to the American faith kept them moving and finally got them to

Council Bluffs, where they met up with the American Fur Company's Rocky Mountain expedition. From there they ventured with varying degrees of discomfort until they arrived at the annual fur traders' rendezvous on 6 July.[26]

On their arrival at the rendezvous it became apparent that the string of coincidences that had brought the little party that far was actually something far more awesome. In perfect harmony with the converging visions and the twin dynamics of unfolding providence, the prophets of these two great revivals were about to meet.[27] Moved by the obvious demonstration of providence that he was witnessing, Spalding wrote the ABCFM's corresponding secretary from the trappers' rendezvous on 8 July 1836: "The Nez Perces Indians on learning that we were with the camp came two days to meet us & received us with great kindness & apparent satisfaction." He went on to say that they had told the Indians that they wanted to install their wives safely at the Hudson's Bay establishment in Walla Walla for the winter while they themselves explored the Indian country to find the best place to set up their mission colony. The Indians, however, were equally moved by the obvious show of providence and were not about to stand for any delays: "To this they would not agree. They wished us to go immediately to their village about 3 days from Walla Walla & not leave them at all."[28] The prophetic process had trapped the participants: the prophets had met, and there was no turning back.

As if in recognition of the process's inexorability, Spalding reported to the board:

> We think it advisable to comply with their wish as far as expedient, to follow them if they do not approach too near the Black Feet for meat, but if they can find meat between here and Fort Hall they will take a more western route consequently a safer one. But to be safe we shall probably hire a pilot to Walla Walla, so that if we find it inexpedient to follow the whole tribe we can take our other course. . . . We shall go to their village probably & if the health of our females demands it, take them to Walla Walla to winter; if not, send there for supplies & settle at once among the Indians.[29]

This was the first of many changes of plan mandated by the overwhelming force of the unfolding prophecies.

The first stop on their roundabout trip to Walla Walla was Fort Hall. Here, they received another sign of providence. According to Spalding, a warm debate took place between the Nez Perce and the Cayuse over the location for the mission, each being anxious to have it in its tribe.[30] This debate prompted the missionaries to reconsider the ABCFM model of a single missionary colony: "On arriving at W[alla] W[alla] we were satisfied with what we could see ourselves & learn from the traders that unless we formed a connecting chain of intercourse & supplies, between this fort & the Flat Head & Nez Perces country the cause of missions would in the end sustain an irreparable loss. To effect this one establishment must be commenced on the WW river."[31]

Confronted with an entirely new situation, the missionaries decided to repair to Fort Vancouver to consult with Hudson's Bay Company Chief Factor John McLaughlin and obtain whatever supplies they needed. They found McLaughlin very helpful and decided the women would remain in his care while the men returned up the Columbia to explore for mission sites. Whitman and Spalding chose two locations, one "on the Walla Walla River about 25 miles from the Fort in the Cayuse so called by Traders or (as they call themselves) Wiiletpoo Country" and the other "in the Nez Perces Country about 100 miles from the former." Between them they decided that Whitman would occupy the post among the Cayuse and that Spalding would take the more pioneer station among the Nez Perce.[32]

Having made this decision, Spalding returned to Vancouver to get building materials and to fetch the women. Meanwhile, Whitman and Gray began the construction of the first mission house on 14 October 1836. By 22 November Spalding had returned with the women, and the Waiilatpu station had been finished sufficiently for the Spaldings and Gray to move on to the site they had selected among the Nez Perce.[33] They arrived 29 November 1836. After a month of hard labor building a mission house in Lapwai, Gray departed for Fort Vancouver, where he was to make arrangements for building the third link in the chain, his own establishment among the Flathead.[34]

Obviously, if the chain of missions was to stretch to all of the Plateau tribes, more missionaries were required. Spalding, in a letter addressed to ABCFM Secretary David Greene, had already requested them, at the same time expressing the expansionistic vision inherent in the new American faith:

> Who will come & possess the *land*, who? Fifty laborers mostly farmers are this day greatly needed to enter the fields all white for the harvest. And unless laborers come forth speedily, the mighty harvest must sink ungathered into the earth. Ah would that we might stay our fears here. These unsuspecting sheep scattered over these hills will not remain long unnoticed by the devouring wolves. Will none from our full churches, none from the Schools of Prophets come to our assistance? Oh ye favored Sons of Zion, Shall these waiting eyes, thick around, some having actually followed us 900 miles watching our every movement, fearful after all they shall lose us, *wait*, & *wait*, & *wait*, till closed in death, & count only *five* weak hearted laborers? Forbid it, Oh those whose right it is to speak with a voice that will be heard, & that will persuade the Fathers of Zion, the young men, the Settled Pastors, to do their duty, to pay their honest debt.[35]

His dedication to obtaining reinforcements was revealed further in the following spring. Spalding felt justified in abandoning the effort to form a Flathead mission in favor of presenting a more powerful case to the board. He therefore ordered Gray to venture back to Boston, where he was to impress upon the board the immediate need for reinforcements and for such sophisticated equipment as grist and sawmill hardware.[36]

There were many among the "favored Sons of Zion" who were ready to "pay their honest debt," but few who were actually qualified seemed to be interested in the domestic variety of heathens. Most preferred more exotic fields like Southeast Africa, Siam, or the Sandwich Islands. The Panic of 1837 made such aspirations unrealistic, however, compelling the Board to turn three previously overseas-bound missionary couples over to Gray to assist in the task of saving the Plateau people. After a disastrous overland trip, a force of nine missionaries, including Gray's new bride Mary Augusta, the Elkana Walkers, the Asa Bowen Smiths, Mr. and Mrs. Cushing Eells, and an unmarried mechanic named Cornelius Rogers, arrived on the Plateau at the end of August 1838.[37]

With the arrival of this party and the many that would follow, it appeared that the Plateau prophecy was working perfectly. Yet, the Indian prophecy had not prepared the Plateau people for the fact that their religious plea had been received as a metaphor in a very different sacred structure.[38] These newly arrived teachers were living in their own world and had prophetic goals that had been firmly fixed through their own individual revitalizations.

Testifying to his conversion in a letter to the ABCFM, Spalding had reported a radical revitalization: "[I] lived a very wicked life among wicked men till the age of 22 when God in great mercy reared me from the depths of sin & brought me, as I hope, into his kingdom, ignorant indeed & poor & with feeble health."[39] In a similar vein, Whitman had reported that "the summer after I was sixteen . . . I was awakened to a sense of my sin and danger and brought by Divine grace to rely on the Lord Jesus for compassion[?] and Salvation," and his fiancée had written that she, too, had undergone a radical transformation during "a precious revival of religion" in Prattsburg in 1819. In fact, all the ABCFM missionaries reported similar experiences.[40]

As a result of their conversion experiences, the missionaries were rendered incapable of dealing objectively with situations. They were, in fact, transformed into Leon Festinger's "man with a conviction":

> A man with a conviction is a hard man to change. Tell him you disagree and he turns away. Show him facts or figures and he questions your sources. Appeal to logic and he fails to see your point.
>
> We have all experienced the futility of trying to change a strong conviction, especially if the convinced person has some invest-

ment in his belief. We are familiar with the variety of ingenious defenses with which people protect their convictions, managing to keep them unscathed through the most devastating attacks.

But man's resourcefulness goes beyond simply protecting a belief. Suppose an individual believes something with his whole heart; suppose further that he has a commitment to this belief, that he has taken irrevocable actions because of it; finally, suppose that he is presented with evidence, unequivocal and undeniable evidence, that his belief is wrong: what will happen? The individual will frequently emerge, not only unshaken, but even more convinced of the truth of his beliefs than ever before. Indeed, he may even show a new fervor about convincing and converting other people to his view.[41]

It must be remembered that the faith to which the missionaries owed their conviction and to which they had made an existential commitment was a syncretic blending of theology and xenophobic patriotism and that American culture, as they defined it, was as much an aspect of their faith as the sacraments or perhaps even the Scriptures. Thus these reborn Americans were totally incapable of looking at Indian cultures objectively; even in the field viewing the cultures firsthand, they could not learn from their experiences.[42] This ethnocentricity was reflected in the missionaries refusal even to investigate the cultures they were invading.[43]

From the missionaries' perspective, it appeared that the Indians were struggling to accept God's offer of grace and salvation but were being led by their primitive—and by implication, evil—ways to reject God. Peering at the world through this prism of prejudice, Spalding and Whitman saw clearly that, in order to carry out God's will, they needed to concentrate not on imparting Christian knowledge as much as on removing pagan ignorance. As Spalding put it, "While we point them with one hand to the Lamb of God which taketh away the sins of the world, we believe it to be *equally* our duty to point with the other to the hoe."[44] Thus were the Indians to be made into the hardworking yeoman farmers that the new syncretic American faith associated with a true Christian life.[45]

Armed with this peculiarly militant cultural chauvinism, the Protestant missionaries immediately set about trying to strip the Indians of every vestige of their normal way of life. As predicted in both the white and Indian prophecies, the missionaries were going to teach the Indians everything; in the process, the Indian world would fall to pieces.

CHAPTER 7

The Converging
Millennia

The Plateau Indians and the Protestant missionaries each had a similar goal. From the Indian perspective, they were to attend the lessons of the missionaries, learn everything, and then their world would come to an end. This was in accord with the Protestant vision, the goal of which was to convert the Indians so as to enlist them into God's forces at Armageddon while at the same time proving America's worthiness as the scene for the expected millennium. This seeming convergence kept both groups occupied in trying to live up to the words of their prophets in order to bring about their separately conceived millennia.

Their role as the bearers of the needed information gave the missionaries the more active part in the unfolding drama, and they played it with an almost hysterical vigor. Contributing to the hysteria was the fact that perceptions of Indian damnation growing out of the Arminian theology associated with the Second Great Awakening caused the missionaries very real spiritual discomfort. Complaining of a delay in taking the field, Asa Bowen Smith gave expression to this pain:

> But the fact that the heathen is in a perishing condition is the great affecting fact. Their condition there is wretched in the extreme: but what is infinitely more affecting, they dishonor God, die in their sins, & are lost. While I am detained here, souls are washing into a wretched eternity beyond the reach of my influence. If I were there, I might under God be the means of saving some of them. This is a painful fact & how can I avoid being anxious to be in the field?[1]

The missionaries' anxiety level rose at the arrival of their most feared enemies. In October 1838 Elkana Walker reported that "the emissaries of the man of sin have made their way to this country. What will be the effect we cannot tell. At this place [Waiilatpu] they made a great display performing high Mass. Some of the Indians were pleased with it and others were disgusted."[2] Walker went on to report that the priests were to confine their missionary activities to the already Catholic Canadian and Indian Hudson's Bay Company employees but confided, "We all know their feeling: the end justifies the means. Our only hope is in the Lord through the shining prejudice there exists in the minds of most of the gentlemen against Popery."[3]

The two priests, Francis Norbert Blanchet and Modeste Demers, had indeed been assigned by the bishop of Quebec to minister to a settlement on the Willamette River, but according to their letter of appointment, the priests were to consider, as their first object, "to withdraw from barbarity and disorders which it produces, the Indians scattered in that country." As a result, Demers embarked on an almost two-month-long crusade among the tribes around Colville, those at Okanagon, and the natives at Walla Walla, all "to the great joy of the assembled Indians."[4]

The presence of these "emissaries of the man of sin" aroused the missionaries' greatest fears. These fears, combined with spiritual anxiety over Indian damnation, made the Protestants feel compelled to launch a full-scale assault on the social and economic structure of Plateau life. As Spalding expressed his designs in a letter to friends back home, "A few of us . . . feel it to be an unyielding duty to do all we can with our limited means, & with a proper regard to our more appropriate labor as teachers & preachers, to call in as it were, the people from their wandering mode of living & settle them upon their lands." He explained that there were two primary reasons for this conclusion. The first was humanitarian: "On arriving in this country we found this people in a most pitiable situation as it respects the means of subsistence, depending entirely on roots fish & game. To obtain these precarious sources, requires them to be constantly on the move & moreover, requires an intensity of labor which but few white people could endure." For the second, Spalding offered the observation "Does not all history and experience show us that a people in such circumstances, can not be essentially benefitted by religious instruction."[5]

The combination of the missionaries' profound anxieties and their inability to understand the complicated society they sought to civilize resulted in outrageously unrealistic expectations of how long this process would take. As Robert Berkhofer has observed, these expectations could not be achieved using current psychological conditioning techniques, much less the primitive techniques available to nineteenth-century missionaries.[6] Spalding gave voice to this unrealistic attitude: "Through the grace of God I expect in a few years this people will have no occasion to leave for the hills & plains, the rivers & mountains for provisions, at least for any great length of time."[7]

To meet this schedule, the missionaries adopted increasingly radical methods, the best example being the great dog slaughter. As reported by Smith, Spalding and Whitman "were in such haste to introduce all the arts of civilization among the Indians at the very onset, they encumbered themselves with sheep; but the camp was so full of dogs that the poor harmless sheep could have no peace but were in danger of being destroyed at once. . . . The Indians were fond of their dogs & unwilling to give them up & there was great excitement throughout the camp." Spalding's solution was to offer a bounty for killing the people's pets, a job that some of his converts undertook, "tho' at the risk of getting the hate of their own people."[8]

When bribery proved insufficient to induce the people to become civilized, Spalding turned to threats and finally to physical violence, not only toward the offensive dogs, but toward their masters. As Smith went on to report:

> In Mr. Spalding's management with the Indians, he has been accustomed to force them to his measures. For a time when they did not act to suit him he would occasionally threaten to leave them, but when they saw that he had no such intention, such threats began to lose their effect. He has been much in the habit of using the whip or causing it to be used upon the people. . . . He has justified himself in this course to the Indians from the example of Christ in making a scourge of small cords & driving the people from the temple.[9]

That the proud people who occupied the Plateau permitted Spalding to treat them in such a manner demonstrates the power of their revitalization and the intensity of their investment in the prophesied course of events. Like their Protestant counterparts, they were incapable of understanding the true situation; even in the face of such humiliating treatment, they remained committed to learning everything from the missionaries. Yet, countervailing pressures were beginning to build, leading some with less invested to doubt the wisdom of following the prophecy.

One major source of dissonance was the tension between the Protestant and Catholic missionaries. Although Blanchet and Demers's 1838 crusade had created a great stir among the Plateau Indians, the temporary nature of Demers's mission made it no great threat to the Protestants and certainly of little value to the natives. But within a year Pierre Jean de Smet had made his first trip to the Plateau. "My mission was one of investigation and inquiry," he wrote, "merely a preparatory visit—yet such were the admirable dispositions of these poor people—so perfectly were their hearts prepared by the action of divine grace, that we can date from this moment, the conversion of the nation." Like

Whitman before him, de Smet was spurred by the overwhelming evidence of providence. He rushed back to civilization, where he rounded up two additional priests and three lay brothers, organized them into an expedition, and arranged to depart in the following spring.[10]

The party left St. Louis on 30 April 1841. Boating as far as they could, the fathers left the river and joined an overland party headed by the long-time mountain man Andrew Drips, who guided them as far as the Beaverhead Valley. Here they encountered a large Flathead party, which took them to the Bitter Root Valley at the very heart of Flathead country. There the missionaries selected a likely spot for building the master link in a projected chain of Plateau missions and began work on 24 September on what was to be called St. Mary's.[11]

To realize this chain, de Smet set out to round up additional troops and was most successful. In 1843 Fathers de Vos and Hoeken arrived with three lay brothers from St. Louis. Then, in 1844, de Smet returned from Europe with four priests and six Sisters of Notre Dame, Namur.[12] "The year 1844 may be considered as a most providential year for the Oregon Missions," the Sisters of Notre Dame reported; and by the end of the following year, according to Jesuit historian William Norbert Bischoff, the series of missions was well established.[13]

While all of this may have appeared "providential" to the Catholics, to reborn Protestants like Spalding and Gray it only served as proof of the international Romanist conspiracy. As for the Indians, their prophecies had not prepared them for competing truths, yet they suddenly found themselves in the middle of a propaganda war between two Christian faiths, each of which used its Indian charges as pawns in a continuing game of sectarian chess.

The best illustration of this war between the faiths is the battle of the "ladders." This struggle began innocently enough when Father Blanchet realized that the Indians had difficulty understanding the European concept of time. He decided that a graphic representation of church history would acquaint his Indian students with a linear scheme of chronology. Therefore, in 1839, he had drawn up a chart consisting of forty lines followed by thirty-three dots followed by eighteen more lines and thirty-nine more dots. These markings represented the forty centuries before Christ, the thirty-three years of his life, the eighteen centuries since the crucifixion, and the thirty-nine years of the current century to 1839.[14]

From this bare outline, a whole graphic tradition arose in which each line and dot were illustrated with scenes from the Bible or from church history. Needless to say, such Protestant patriarchs as Luther, Calvin, and Henry VIII were depicted as fomenters of error headed for damnation. Whitman passed on a description of one of these ladders which, he said, "represents all protestants as the whithered ends of the several branches of the Papacy falling down off into infernal society & flames as represented at the bottom." According to Spalding, such depictions were not limited to Protestant church fathers. He supposedly boasted some years later that both he and Whitman were similarly singled out for illustration on a Catholic ladder he had seen.[15]

Spalding, who already had a predilection for the use of graphics, chose to meet the Catholic threat with a propaganda campaign of his own, a task for which his years as a student of Lyman Beecher had prepared him well. He explained his strategy to David Greene in such excruciating detail that the letter warrants quoting at length:

> To meet this attack I have planèd [sic] & Mrs. S[palding] has drawn & painted a chart about 6 feet long & 2 wide containing two ways, one narrow & one broad. After representing briefly some of the important events of the world before the christian era & the crucifixion of Christ, I come to Paul, whom I represent as pointing to one who has turned off from the narrow way where he has left his wife & children & with black gown & a cross in his hand is just entering the Broad Road.
>
> A few of Paul's prophecies concerning the man of sin are translated & printed as proceeding from his mouth such as he shall forbid to marry etc. After he has left his wife & entered the Broad Road, he is represented as the Pope with a sword in one hand & torch or fagot in the other, a king kissing one foot & a bishop

the other. Further up he is represented with 5 children by his side & again as receiving the bleeding head of Admiral Coligny who was beheaded at the great slaughter of St. Bartholomew & has his head sent by Charles IX to the Pope who ordered public thanks to be given to Charles & a jubilee to be proclaimed throughout France.

Boniface IX & Benedict XIII are represented as contending with deadly weapons. Tetzel receiving a sum of money from a young man whose father has escaped hell all but one of his feet, is represented. A Nunnery is drawn from which a young priest has come out & is paying 18s to get the sin of Fornication pardoned according to "tasa camarae Apostolicae" of the Chancery court of Rome.

The lifeless body of a father killed by his own son for money, is represented with the mother & sisters weeping on the bleeding corpse, & at a little distance the murderer before a priest receiving pardon for 10s 6d according to the same book. Some of those burnt in queen Mary's reign are drawn, the Burning of Bibles in the N of N.Y. State is drawn. Luther is represented as leaving the Broad road and returning to the narrow way. The end of the Man of Sin is represented by his falling back into hell at the approach of the Lord Jesus Christ who is coming in the clouds of heaven with his holy angels.[16]

How successful this technique was for teaching ecclesiastical history is open to question, but it was an excellent means of conveying prejudice. As Whitman testified concerning the Catholic ladder, "The possession of one of these manuscripts by an Indian binds him not to hear any more the instruction of Protestants so far as my observation can prove."[17] A Catholic missionary, Father Joseph Caltado, later ascribed similar powers to the Protestant ladders, asserting that while Spalding "made few converts . . . still he succeeded in poisening their minds against the Catholic religion."[18]

In addition to the religious battle between the Catholics and Protestants, an internal sectarian conflict was straining the Protestant mission to the breaking point. The ABCFM was a hybrid creature. Conceived under the 1801 Plan of Union, it incorporated both Presbyterian and Congregationalist missionaries.

Even when doctrinal schisms destroyed the plan in 1837, the ABCFM struggled on. Unfortunately, adherents of the two Protestant sects clashed openly the field.[19]

There had been tension among the various members of the ABCFM mission since the transportation mix-up at St. Louis in 1836. These tensions were greatly aggravated when the reinforcement arrived late in 1838, and by 1840 the combination of doctrinal differences and deep-seated personal animosities had resulted in festering discontent.[20] This dissatisfaction was expressed in some thirty thousand words of criticism from Smith to the board in that year, and during the same period, Gray wrote three critical missives and Whitman, one. This open war within the mission must have been just as confusing to the millennium-anticipating Indians as the battle with the Catholics, perhaps more so.[21]

Even more likely to disturb the Indians than these influences was the sudden upturn in the number of whites entering the area. Ever since the great Methodist invasion of 1838, settlers had been drifting into the Oregon country, but from 1841 on, the numbers increased dramatically. Reporting the arrival of a party of 112 in June 1842, Federal Indian Commissioner Elijah White noted that "great interest was excited; but they afterwards poured in in such numbers, that it was difficult to entertain them, saying nothing of the novelty being lost."[22]

Though it may seem antithetical (and would eventually prove dangerous) to the missionaries' work with the Indians, they were in favor of this immigration and, to some degree, responsible for it. After all, one of Spalding's first acts upon arriving in the field had been to issue a call for reinforcements. His call was not, however, a manifestation of cynical American imperialism. In fact, like his superiors, Spalding was leery of unbridled American expansion and convinced of its inevitable ill effects on the Indians. As he wrote to Greene, "The overwhelming flood of annihilation continues to roll down upon these defenceless hunted immortals, from the snow capped mountains of Avarice, Intemperance, Licentiousness, Infidelity & nameless other sins, rendering every effort to benefit these tribes almost useless."[23] At the same time, however, there was a threefold purpose in attempting to attract settlers.

First, the missionaries believed that the best way to instruct the Indians in the civilized arts was by example. Pious farmers would provide such an example while demonstrating, through their comfortable and increasingly prosperous lifestyle, the superiority of white civilization.[24] Second, the area in which the missions were located was then jointly occupied by the United States and Great Britain. Given the syncretic nature of the missionaries' faith, they tended to favor enterprises that would enhance America's claim to the territory, including increasing the American population. Although there is little discussion of this issue in the primary documents, it would appear that it did figure in the missionaries' thinking.[25] The third and probably most important purpose was financial. As Spalding explained in a letter advocating to the board a settlement in the Cowlitz area:

> I give this field a prominant place among many others that might be mentioned in this part of the world for the following reasons. An establishment here would be of incalculable benefit to all establishments in the Columbia or west of the Mountains. & also to our Missions on the Sandwich Islands, the way of furnishing the essential supplies which must now be obtained at a greater or lesser extent from foreign markets [i.e., the British Hudson's Bay Company]. . . . An establishment here might be conducted, i.e., by enterprising, pious, farmers, machanicks, teachers, & Missionaries, might, I think, in a few years render all our missionary establishments in this part of the world nearly independent of foreign aid, & permit the thousands now required to sustain them, to be laid out on other fields.[26]

It is, of course, difficult to gauge how influential such reports were in encouraging immigration to Oregon, but given the wide dissemination of news about the Oregon missions, this influence should not be underestimated.[27] Certainly the Indians saw some correlation, and this, added to other dissonances, gave many of the natives a real sense of foreboding. Insecurity led some of the Indians to question the prophecy and challenge the presence of the whites in their territory, and this resulted in the eruption of violence on several occasions. In August 1842 Spalding reported:

> Doct. Whitman has had his life threatened. Last fall I was called in haste to meet the families (viz. Whitman & Gray) at Fort Walla Walla where they had expected to take shelter from the fury of the natives. Their house had been entered, the door broken in by an axe, which was aimed at Doct. W.'s head, but he avoided the blow and wrested the axe from the Indian & his wife conveyed it from the crowd. Mr. Gray was surrounded in another part of the house & attacked by a hammer which he succeeded in taking from the Indian, a gun was aimed at one of them, but probably was not loaded. Four white men fortunately coming, partly armed, the Indians having accomplished their wish (viz. entering the house as they pleased) retired. . . . The Doct.'s house has since been entered by some 6 or 8 with a war club & ropes, but after a short talk they retired without attempting to use them.[28]

To make matters worse, two months after Spalding's report, Whitman embarked on a trip back to the United States to try to correct a new set of orders forwarded by the ABCFM Prudential Committee but made unnecessary by a negotiated peace between the missionaries. Unfortunately, the Indians, knowing nothing of internal mission affairs, regarded his disappearance with great apprehension. As Narcissa Whitman wrote to Mary Walker concerning the Indian response to Marcus's absence, "Nothing is talked of or has been for the whole winter but War! War! They say they have been told Doct. W. has gone home & is coming back next fall with 50 men to fight them."[29]

Apprehension led to more violence, against the missionaries and all whites passing through the Plateau. Only three days after Whitman's departure, there was another break-in attempt at the Waiilatpu mission. It was foiled by a Hawaiian servant, but Mrs. Whitman was sufficiently unnerved to abandoned the mission and flee to the settlement at The Dalles.[30] This was only the beginning of Indian reprisals. According to Elijah White,

> A few days after this they burned down the mission mill on his premises, with all its appendages and considerable grain, damag-

ing them not less than twelve or fifteen hundred dollars. About the same time Mrs. Spalding was grossly insulted in her own house, and ordered out of it in the absence of her husband. Information reached him of an Indian having stolen his horse near the same time, he hastened to the spot to secure the animal; the rogue had crossed the river; but immediately returning, he presented his loaded gun, cocked, at the breast of Mr. Spalding, abused and menaced as far as possible without shooting him.

In addition to this, some of our own party were robbed openly of considerable property, and some twelve horses were stolen by night.[31]

"All this information coming near the same time" compelled White to do something in his role as Indian sub-agent. He formed a filibustering party and marched toward the Plateau. After a brief visit with Mrs. Whitman at The Dalles, White and his party invaded Waiilatpu, but found the Indians in the vicinity "few and shy." "I thought it best to treat them with reserve," White reported, "but made an appointment to meet the chiefs and tribe on my return." From Waiilatpu the small army pressed on to Lapwai to render justice on the Nez Perce ruffians who had mishandled the Spaldings.[32]

Once there, White, an ex-missionary himself, addressed Spalding's complaint that "there being no law, no one takes any notice of the murderers" and undertook to supply some.[33] White described this Hammurabic accomplishment in his 1 April 1843 report to the commissioner of Indian affairs:

All the chiefs and principal men being present, [I] stated delicately the embarrassed relation existing between whites and Indians in this upper country, by reason of a want of proper organization, or the chiefs' authority not being properly regarded; alluded to some cases of improprieties of young men, not sanctioned by the chiefs and old men; and where the chiefs had been in the wrong, hoped it had principly arisen from imperfectly understanding each other's language or some other excusable cause, especially so far as they were concerned. Advised them, as they were now to some extent prepared, to choose one high chief of the tribe, and acknowledge him as such by universal consent; all and other subordinate chiefs being of equal power, and so many helps to carry out all his lawful requirements, which they were at once to have in writing, in their own language, to regulate their intercourse with whites, and in most cases with themselves. I advised that each chief have five men as a body guard, to execute all their lawful commands.[34]

After considerable debate and eliciting of advice from various members of White's party, the people chose Ellis as their head chief. White was elated with the choice because Ellis had been to the Red River School, where he had learned "reading, speaking, and writing the English language tolerably well."[35]

Having settled the Nez Perce problem to his and Spalding's satisfaction, White returned to Waiilatpu, where "we had many most unpleasant matters to settle with the Keyuse tribe—such as personal abuse to Dr. Whitman and lady, burning the mill, &c. &c." Unfortunately for White's designs, several of the most influential Cayuse leaders were away, and he did not feel that those present could provide a sufficient consensus for the adoption of his laws. So, White "made an engagement to meet them and all the tribe the ensuing new moon of April, to adjust differences, and come to a better understanding."[36]

But spring brought the return of Whitman, and that spurred even greater unrest. The Indians had feared that Whitman was returning with fifty men to make war on the Cayuse. Imagine their surprise when word reached them that the doctor led a party of at least a thousand.[37] Worse, Indian rumor had it that White intended to return from the Willamette at the head of "an armed force to take away their lands & compel them to adopt & enforce laws to regulate their own people & redress the wrongs of the whites."[38]

White reported the spreading hysteria in a message to Washington, D.C.:

I received several communications from missionaries of the interior, some from the Methodists, and those sent out by the American board, representing the indians in the interior as in a great

state of excitement, and under much apprehension from the cir-
cumstance that such number of whites were coming in, as they
were informed, to take possession of their land and country. The
excitement soon became general, both among whites and Indians, in this lower as well as upper district; and such were the constantly floating groundless reports, that much uneasiness was felt,
and some of our citizens were under such a state of apprehen-
sions as to abandon their houses, and place themselves more immediately within the precincts of the colony. As in all such cases,
a variety of opinions were entertained and expressed—some
pleading for me, at the expense of the general government, to
throw up a strong fortification in the centre of the colony, and
furnish the settlers with guns and ammunition, so that we might
be prepared for extremities. Others thought it more advisable for
me to go with an armed force of considerable strength to the
heart and centre of the conspiracy, as it was represented, and if
words will not answer, make powder and balls do it.[39]

Bent on averting war, White assembled a small party and set
out for the upper Columbia. He reported that when he arrived,
"the Indians flocked around me, and inquired after my party,
and could not be persuaded, for some time, but that I had a
large party concealed somewhere near, and only waited to get
them convened, to open a fire upon, and cut them all off at a
blow."[40] After considerable discussion, White finally convinced
the Cayuse that he had no army with him and that his sole mission was to arrange a peace. "They were quite astounded and
much affected, assuring me they had been under strong appre-
hensions, having learned I was soon to visit them with a large
armed party, with hostile intentions, and I actually found them
suffering more from fears of war from the whites, than the
whites from the Indians." In their relief, they agreed to meet
with White upon his return from Lapwai, at which time they
agreed to accept a body of laws and to live in peace with Whitman and the incoming settlers.[41]

With war averted, Indian-white relations settled into relative
peace. But, even though confrontations between the Indians

and white Americans ceased for the moment, the pressure to- ward a final confrontation was unabated. After all, it had been predicted that, when the Indians had learned everything, the world would fall to pieces. By the summer of 1843 the Plateau Indians had very little left to learn.

CHAPTER 8

The World Will Fall
to Pieces

O vert violence on the scale seen in 1843 was not to be repeated for some time, but unsettling developments continued. A major one was the growing flood of whites into the Oregon country. Though there had been a constant flow of immigrants, most had simply passed on, disturbing the Plateau very little. Increasingly, however, immigration was having a more immediate impact on the Plateau itself. Ever since the massive immigration Whitman had led in 1843, his mission station had become a regular recuperation stop for the parties headed toward the Willamette. As Matilda Sager Delaney, herself a refugee who spent several childhood years at the mission, put it, "Dr. Whitman always sent the immigrants on to the Willamette valley as fast as he could; but many were obliged to remain at the Mission on account of their oxen having given out and he had to feed from fifty to seventy-five persons during the winter months."[1] As the proprietor of such an establishment, Whitman obviously had less and less time to spend with his Indian charges at a time when their growing anxiety demanded even greater attention. The Plateau Indians must surely have wondered why, if the Whitmans came as missionaries for them, they devoted so much time to white people?

Another source of Indian anxiety and outright anger was the murder of a Wallawalla named Elijah Hedding. During the winter of 1844-1845 this influential young man had led a party of Plateau Indians to Sutter's Fort in California to trade horses for cattle. While there, a misunderstanding over some stolen horses led to an angry confrontation between Hedding and an unruly American. Anti-Indian prejudices inflamed the dispute and finally resulted in the cold-blooded murder of Hedding. His companions were forced to flee for their lives.[2]

When the party got home and the story of Hedding's murder got around, the Plateau tribes became incensed. The newly appointed head chief of the Nez Perce, Ellis, contacted Elijah White, who reported:

> the Wallawallas, Keyuse, Nez Perce, Spokans, Ponderays and Snakes, were all on terms of amity, and that a portion of the aggrieved party were for raising about two thousand warriors of these formidable tribes, and march to California at once, and nobly revenge themselves on the inhabitants by capture and plunder, enrich themselves upon the spoils; others, not indisposed to the enterprise, wished first to learn how it would be regarded here, and whether we would remain neutral in the affair. A third party were for holding us responsible, as Elijah was killed by an American, and the Americans incensed the Spaniards.[3]

White immediately wrote the upland chiefs "assuring them that I should at once write to the governor of California, to captain Suter [sic.], and to our great chiefs, respecting this matter." While this seems to have settled the matter temporarily, ill feelings lingered among the Plateau people, who often referred to the incident when cataloging white crimes against them.[4]

Also aggravating tensions was a spell of especially inclement weather including temperatures of 30 degrees below zero in the winter of 1846-1847. While the missionaries could not do anything about the weather, their policies exacerbated the ill effects. The policy of discouraging what they regarded as nomadism prevented the Indians from driving their animals to sheltered valleys distant from the mission stations. Since the missionaries could offer no shelter in their buildings for the natives' animals, the Indians lost nearly half of their livestock in that one winter.[5] Also, having been discouraged from pursuing their regular food-gathering round, the Indians were, no doubt, short of dried fish, root bread, and other traditional high-protein foods that the missionaries' grain could not replace.

The resulting dietary deficiencies may have contributed to another source of ill feeling in the following year. According to Drury, many of the immigrants who paused at Whitman's station were "sick and destitute."[6] While Whitman's humanity in caring for such travelers is beyond reproach, the Indians' weakness made them even more susceptible than usual to the diseases carried by these immigrants. As Delaney recalled, "In November of 1847 many immigrants had gathered at the Mission, intending to winter there. Measles had broken out among them and many of the Indians had also become victims of the disease"[7] —so many, in fact, that nearly half of the Indian population around Waiilatpu died of the ailment in a matter of weeks.[8]

Such decimation caused the accumulated anxieties of the Indians to metamorphose into a specific fear. According to the testimony of the principal Cayuse chiefs, "a young Indian, who understands English and who slept in Dr. Whitman's room heard the Doctor, his wife, and Mr. Spalding express their desire of possessing the Indian lands and their animals. He also states that Mr. Spalding had said to the Doctor: a 'Hurry give Medicines to the Indians, that they may soon die.'"[9] It was night of 26 November 1847. Spalding had come to Waiilatpu that day to discuss pressing mission business. Most pressing was the high rate of Indian mortality (197 Cayuse had died in that month alone) and the future of the mission should all of the Cayuse die.[10]

While the causes of the death of Elijah Hedding and the awful weather were perhaps debatable, every Indian on the Plateau knew that disease was the result of either malevolence or spiritual transgression. In either case, the missionaries were responsible. Suddenly, the cause of all of the Indians' problems became clear: "For several years past, they had to deplore the death of their children and . . . they according to these reports were led to believe that the whites had undertaken to kill them all."[11]

On the day after their evil wizardry was revealed, Whitman and Spalding left Waiilatpu to dispense medicine among the Umatilla. The missionaries' absence and the new intelligence concerning the whites' evil magic led to a crisis among the Cayuse. The prophet cult had promised that, when the Indians learned everything, there would be universal life. Faced instead with the real possibility of universal death, the Cayuse decided they had learned enough from the Protestant missionaries, and they resolved to defend themselves from the whites' shamanism. In the absence of a shaman more powerful than Whitman and Spalding, the only alternative was to remove the evil magicians. The Indian who reported the Whitman-Spalding conversation had, indeed, warned "If you do not kill the Doctor soon you will all be dead before spring."[12]

The clerics had intended to be gone through Sunday, 28 November, but according to Delaney, "The Doctor was very worried because there were so many sick at his Mission, having ten of his own family down and Mrs. Whitman much alarmed about the Children. Some of them were very low—especially my sister Louise and Helen Marr Meek. Leaving Mr. Spalding at Umatilla, the Doctor started for home."[13] While Whitman was gone another nine Cayuse had died, three of whom had not yet been buried by the time of his return. Unaware that he would be joining them shortly, Whitman bade farewell to these three souls on the morning of the twenty-ninth. Immediately after the ceremony, Whitman was confronted in the mission kitchen, and in prescribed fashion, his evil was excised by an axe blow that crushed his skull.[14]

Whitman was only the first of some thirteen white people who would die to eliminate the evil from the Plateau. In the two-day killing spree, both Whitmans, their schoolmaster, several immigrant fathers, and two of the Sager children were slaughtered. The Indians also intended to kill Whitman's co-conspirator when he returned from the Umatilla, but good fortune and Father J. B. A. Brouillet intervened. Meeting Spalding on the road to Waiilatpu, the priest informed him of the massacre, warned him that his head was also in peril, gave him some food, and told him to flee while he could.[15]

Affected no doubt by Brouillet's gesture and fearful for his own life, Spalding temporarily abandoned his anti-Catholicism and wrote a moving letter to Augustine Blanchet, bishop of the Catholic diocese centered at Nesqually and brother of his ex-adversary Francis Blanchet: "Through the astonishing mercy of God, the hand of our merciful God brought me to my family, after 6 days and nights from the time my dear friend furnished me with provisions and I escaped from the Indians." Still, Spalding was only provisionally safe. As he went on to explain to Blanchet, "The Nez Perce held a meeting yesterday; they pledged to protect us from the Cayuse if we would prevent the Americans from coming up to avenge the murders. This we have pledged to do, and for this we beg for the sake of our lives at this place and at Mr. Walker's." "By all means keep quiet," he concluded, "send no war report, send nothing but proposals of peace. They say they have buried the death of the Walla Walla Chief's son killed in California they wish to bury this offense."[16]

Like their Nez Perce neighbors, the Cayuse also had a set of demands and a group of hostages to use for leverage. The Cayuse chiefs sent their six demands through Bishop Blanchet, who reported them to Governor George Abernethy:

> The same chiefs ask at present,
> 1st. That the Americans may not go to war with the Cayuses.
> 2nd. That they may forget the lately commited murders, as the Cayuses will forget the murder of the son of the great Chief of Walla Walla, commited in California.
> 3rd. That two or three great men may come up to conclude peace.
> 4th. That as soon as these great men have arrived and concluded peace, they may take with them all the women and children.
> 5th. They give assurance that they will not harm the Americans before the arrival of these three great men.
> 6th. They ask that the Americans may not travel any more

through their country, as their young men might do them harm.[17]

The Cayuse did not know that the chief factor at Fort Vancouver had already dispatched a peace commission under the leadership of the veteran Hudson's Bay man Peter Skene Ogden. In fact, Ogden and his company arrived only two days after the council with Blanchet. According to H. H. Bancroft, Ogden made a speech to the assembled chiefs in which he stressed that, while the British and Americans were "of a different nation," they were "of the same color, speak the same language, and worship the same God." Thereupon Ogden reminded the Indians that the Hudson's Bay Company was their primary source for guns, ammunition, and other such commodities and warned them that the traders felt very badly about the death of Whitman and the others. He then concluded, "If you wish it, on my return, I will see what can be done for you; but I do not promise to prevent war. Deliver me the prisoners to return to their friends, and I will pay you a ransom. That is all."[18]

Possibly remorseful over the murders and undoubtedly frightened by Ogden's tone, the Cayuse acceded to the trader's offer, accepting a cargo of blankets, shirts, guns, ammunition, tobacco, and flints in exchange for the hostages. Meanwhile, the Nez Perce had kept Spalding and his family safe. Upon hearing about the deal between Ogden and the Cayuse, they resolved to free their prisoners as well. Finally, on 1 January 1848 the Spaldings were escorted by a party of friendly Nez Perces to Fort Walla Walla, where they were reunited with their daughter and the other survivors of Waiilatpu.[19]

It was just as well that Ogden had made no promises concerning peace. By the time of Spalding's release, a militia company from the Willamette had already reached The Dalles, and another was being formed which was to march up river soon after. In the war that followed, the primary form of military action was an exchange of horse or cattle rustling with a few shots fired in the process, a type of warfare at which the Cayuse excelled. They managed to delay the American force long enough for the parties it sought to escape from the area. This accomplished, the situation settled into an uneasy stalemate.[20]

Though the Cayuse War accomplished nothing for either side, it did mark the beginning of the Plateau Indian apocalypse. Along with the massacre, the war brought an end to the process that had begun with the Spokan and other prophecies nearly a century and a half before. The Cayuse had decided that they had learned enough from the "different kind of man" and had expelled him. The Americans in Oregon had been forced to alter their millennial expectations as well. They decided that the Indians' act of war had removed the Plateau dwellers from the roll of God's chosen. The dynamics of the two-way evangelical Manifest Destiny officially ceased when Indian Superintendent H. A. G. Lee closed the interior to missionaries of all callings.[21]

For nearly three-quarters of a century the relationship between the Plateau Indians and the Americans had been based on the role that each occupied in the millenarian expectations of the other. Suddenly neither occupied a favored place in the other's world view. As a result, the entire basis for Indian-white relations collapsed. Until the Whitman Massacre, the rights of the Indians had been upheld by America's missionary representatives. They had been convinced that the Indians, once converted, would settle on small tracts, freeing the majority of the Plateau for white settlement. Having apostatized, however, the Indians had confounded this expectation, opening themselves up to forced consolidation and dispossession.

It did not take long for the Americans to announce this changed policy. Only eight months after the massacre, Superintendent Lee had the following edict published in the *Oregon Spectator*:

> In consideration of the barbarous and insufferable conduct of the Cayuse Indians, as portrayed in the massacre of the American families at Waiilatpu, and the subsequent course of hostilities against the Americans generally; and with a view to inflict upon them a just and proper punishment, as well as to secure and protect our fellow citizens, immigrating from the United States to this territory, against a course of reckless aggressions so long and

uniformly practiced upon them by said Cayuse Indians: after con-
sideration with His Excellency, Geo. Abernethy, Gov. O. [regon]
T.[erritory], and with his advice and consent, I, H. A. G.
Lee, Superin't of Indian Affairs, hereby declare the territory of
said Cayuse Indians forfeited by them, and justly subject to be
occupied and held by American citizens, resident in Oregon.[22]

Considering the unsettled state of affairs in the interior, it is not
surprising that Americans did not rush in to take over the newly
opened lands. Even after things quieted down, there was no
great demand for the Cayuse's land, making the new status of
the Indians of little immediate consequence. The precedent
had, however, been set.

Seven years after Lee's announcement, the governor of Washington Territory capitalized on the opportunity. Like many of
his predecessors on the Plateau, Isaac I. Stevens was a man with
a vision — a vision of a northern transcontinental railroad with
its western terminus on Puget Sound. Like so many other vi-
sionaries, he managed to work his way into a position from
which he could be an active agent in the development of his pet
project. In addition to being appointed territorial governor for
Washington and superintendent of Indian affairs, Stevens was
also appointed by War Secretary Jefferson Davis to head the survey for the northern railroad route. Not recognizing any
conflicts of interest, Stevens gleefully used all three positions to
enhance his power and forward his dream.[23]

As with all railroad projects, it was necessary to acquire a sufficient right-of-way to accommodate the tracks and to provide in-
centives for any company that might take it up. Since Stevens's
projected route followed the Oregon Trail across the Plateau,
the governor donned his Indian superintendent hat and set out
to make treaties with all of the Plateau tribes. According to Andrew Jackson Splawn, who interviewed "many of their old chiefs
and warriors,"

> Word went out to all the tribes of the Northwest that the Father
> in Washington, D.C., wanted their lands for the white men and
> that a great white chief was even now on his way out to buy them;

and that, moreover, if they refused to sell, soldiers would be sent to drive them off and seize the lands. Such news naturally aroused the indignation of every tribe in Washington Territory, creating a strong prejudice against Governor Stevens, so that, upon his arrival, he was regarded with the suspicion that would attach to a man who had come to take from them their country. This was the situation at the beginning of 1854.[24]

At that time, the most powerful of the Yakima chiefs, Kamiakin, reminded his people of the old prophecy but added that people who had been in California reported that the Indians there were dying off and that in his own travels he had witnessed the reduction of the tribes of the Willamette Valley. He then pointed out that if whites were allowed to settle on the Plateau, the same would surely happen to them. He therefore urged the assembled Indians to meet Stevens with resistance. "If they take our lands," he is reported to have said, "their trails will be marked with blood."[25]

Kamiakin then called up the Plateau military task group. Based on the information extracted in his many interviews, Splawn wrote the following account of Kamiakin's effort:

> Couriers were sent speeding to the south at once to spread out among the different nations, while Skloom, with another Yakima, went to the Warm Springs, Des Chutes, Tyghs and Was-co-pams, with the intention also of visiting the Klickitats on their return to Yakima.
>
> Ka-mi-akin returned to the Ahtanum alone. Shortly after, Ow-hi, Quil-ten-e-nock, Moses and Qual-chan arrived and were informed of the result of his meeting with Pe-peu-mox-mox and Looking Glass. The Yakima chief urged them to busy themselves in the north, east and west, in the work Skloom was doing in the Des Chutes country and the couriers in the south.
>
> These bold men were pleased with the plan and eager for action. An understanding was soon reached. Quil-ten-e-nock and Moses were to go north; Qual-chan to Puget Sound to meet Leschi and others who would look after that region; while Ka-mi-akin and Ow-hi would go east.
>
> Well equipped with tough and wiry horses, and a few men along to look after them, they were soon on their respective ways,

full of hope. To the head men of each tribe they dwelt on the menace in the words of Governor Stevens and insisted that their only hope was to stand together. If soldiers were sent into any part of the Indian country and a battle fought, it should be the signal for a general uprising from every quarter.[26]

In the summer of 1854 Kamiakin's efforts were rewarded. According to Splawn, every influential Indian leader on the Plateau had heeded the messengers; they came together for a five-day council in the Grand Ronde Valley. All agreed that the situation was grave and pondered the best way of dealing with it. The overwhelming majority preferred not even to meet with Stevens; instead they advocated that his entry into the country serve as a signal for war. Three chiefs, however, advised that the Indians should at least hear out the whites' arguments, thereby avoiding an unnecessary war.[27] Two of these three were old actors in the now questionable prophecy. One was Spokan Garry, the Indian who had brought the Christian message from the Red River School to the Plateau. The second was Hol-lol-sote-tote, who, as a young man, had carried Garry's message to the Nez Perce and Flathead, paving the way for the delegation of 1831. Now, under the name Lawyer, Hol-lol-sote-tote had replaced the recently deceased Ellis as the white-appointed head chief of the entire Nez Perce nation.[28]

In the ensuing debate a compromise solution was reached that satisfied all. They concluded to mark the boundaries of the different tribes so that each chief could rise in council, claim his boundaries, and ask that the land be made a reservation for his people. Then there would be no lands for sale, the council would fail, and at the same time Lawyer and Garry's stipulations would be met. Each leader then marked out his claim and the grand alliance council adjourned to await Stevens's next move.[29]

In the following spring, Stevens sent James Doty, then acting special agent to the Blackfeet, to the Plateau to arrange an inter-tribal treaty council. Having laid their plans and feeling assured of success, Kamiakin and the other chiefs readily consented to meet with Stevens on 20 May 1855 in the Walla Walla country. Even Lawyer, who had been excluded from the decision making, was looking forward to the session. In the hope that the belief system in which he had played so large a role and to which he had dedicated himself totally might be resurrected, Lawyer had tipped off Stevens and his party about the intertribal agreement.[30]

It took over a week for all of the parties involved to assemble. Finally, however, the assembly was officially convened on 30 May 1855. Working on Lawyer's information and therefore anticipating the chiefs' strategy, Stevens and Oregon Indian Superintendent Joel Palmer assiduously avoided any reference to details, preferring to utter platitudes about the Great Father's concern for the Indians and outlining the many gifts he wanted to give them. This palaver continued for two days, after which the Indians asked for a one-day continuance to consider what they had heard.[31]

The council reopened on 2 June. Stevens asked the Indians for their response to his proposals. After a couple of nondescript speeches, Wallawalla chief Peo-peo-mox-mox took the floor. Recalling the murder of his son Elijah Hedding in California, the chief railed about white duplicity and demanded that the commissioners get specific and then give the Indians sufficient time to consider the information before requiring any kind of decision. Still playing it close to the vest, Stevens chose to reveal nothing. He adjourned the meeting for the day.[32]

When the council reopened, Lawyer immediately stood and gave a speech expressing his enduring friendship for the whites and his confidence in their honesty. This speech marked the first public defection from the Grand Ronde agreement. While Lawyer's action could not have been totally unexpected, the other chiefs must suddenly have realized that, with the economic and spiritual ties altered by the missionaries' influence, the system could not hold up. In any case, they began to give up hope. Peo-peo-mox-mox was literally speechless, and Kamiakin's only response was a rather hopeless statement: "I have been afraid of the white man their doings are different from ours. Your chiefs are good. Perhaps you have spoken straight, that your children will do what is right, let them do as they have promised."[33]

Seeing the two strongest leaders of the Grand Ronde alliance waver caused the whole structure to begin breaking down. As the day wore on, more and more Indians spoke up, but none of them made any reference to the boundary lines agreed upon the previous summer. Instead, they all seemed interested in getting as much for their own people as possible, regardless of the larger cost.[34] Sensing that he now had the upper hand, Stevens chose this moment to reveal that instead of granting each tribe its own reservation, there were to be only two tracts set aside: one in Nez Perce country to house the Nez Perce, Cayuse, Umatilla, and Wallawalla; one in the Yakima Valley for the Yakima, Klickitat, Palouse, and the rest of the Plateau tribes. As soon as he finished he hurriedly closed the meeting before the full impact of his words could register.[35] The next day was spent explaining the boundaries of the proposed reservations and how much the government intended to give the Indians for the lands they ceded. After ingesting all of this information, the Indians announced they would rather not meet on the following day but they might have something to say on the seventh.[36]

When Stevens reconvened the council on 7 June, things immediately began to break his way. Lawyer, the first respondent Stevens recognized, gave a long speech recounting in glowing terms the history of the relations between his people and the whites. He then agreed to accept the treaty exactly as proposed.[37] With this wedge successfully driven, Palmer immediately stood up and announced that the commissioners had changed their minds and that the Nez Perce would not have to share their reservation with the Wallawalla, Cayuse, and Umatilla but each of these tribes could have its own reservation placed in such a way that none of them would have to relocate.[38]

Seeing Lawyer rewarded for his defection and being offered their own reservations pushed the Wallawalla, Cayuse, and Umatilla chiefs into Stevens's trap. Even Peo-peo-mox-mox was finally swayed by the promise of money, a house, oxen, wagons, plows, and an annual salary of five hundred dollars. Kamiakin was still unshaken in his opposition, but he had been effectively isolated.[39] His isolation was not, however, to last for long. The Nez Perce war leader, Looking Glass, had just returned from the buffalo country and hurried to Walla Walla, arriving on 9 June. After an angry confrontation with his people over their defection, Looking Glass returned to the Grand Ronde formula and demanded the territory originally agreed to by the allied tribes.[40]

This switch rocked Stevens's well-constructed and well-executed strategy. The Nez Perce immediately formed their own council to make a difficult decision: they could choose a comfortable compromise with the assurance of keeping their own lands, or they could accept Looking Glass's demand and preserve the traditional scheme of mutual support and cooperation and in so doing, perhaps lose everything. In a protracted meeting the tribe finally decided that the safer course was the most attractive. They affirmed their support for Lawyer and abandoned the Indian world for the white one.[41]

Peo-peo-mox-mox and his fellow chiefs also decided not to risk their gains and signed the treaty. The Wallawalla chief then met with Kamiakin to try to change the Yakima's mind. It is not known what was said, but Peo-peo-mox-mox may have impressed upon Kamiakin that, without Nez Perce military aid, any resistance would be futile. Whatever was said deflated Kamiakin's spirits so much that he, too, agreed to make his mark on the paper.[42] All the tribes had thus signed, giving Stevens his right-of-way and much, much more. According to Splawn's figures, the Yakima lost a total of twenty-nine thousand square miles, and the Wallawalla, Cayuse, and Umatilla lost all of their holdings in Oregon, retaining only a small reserve on the Washington side of the Columbia. Their strategic defection earned a much better deal for the Nez Perce. They sacrificed only a narrow strip of their own land, but they signed away the entire homeland of their Palouse neighbors.[43]

Stevens's victory was more than just a political defeat for the Plateau people. Always before the defensive Plateau task group had held together in the face of its enemies. Now the bonds had been broken, and each tribe scrambled and contended to get as much for itself as possible, regardless of the social and spiritual consequences for the Plateau system. The Plateau people had finally learned the ultimate lesson from the white men, and their world had fallen to pieces.

Epilogue

The world may have fallen to pieces, but no happy millennium followed, only more fragmentation and division. The tactics Stevens pioneered at the Walla Walla conference continued to serve the whites well in the balance of their dealings with the Plateau tribes. In any crisis the whites' first move was to divide the tribes against each other to prevent reunification of the defensive Plateau military and diplomatic task group. Each time, the effect was the same: the ties that structured Indian life on the Plateau were cut back a little further.

As serious as it was, the diplomatic effect of this strategy was almost insignificant compared with this destruction of ties. Everything on the Plateau depended on the relationships between the groups. The identity of each village, band, tribe, linguistic group, and even of each individual depended on the web of relationships defined by the patterns of mutual cooperation, assistance, and trade. These relationships, in turn, depended on a shared metaphysical reality in which all participated. In abandoning the shared prophetic vision, the Cayuse had taken the first step in dissolving the shared reality. With the prophecies went the revitalized mazeway that had held the Indian world together in the face of disruptive change. As each group defected and grabbed for whatever they could, they defined themselves out of the traditional Indian world and into the world of the white invaders. With that, the Indian world literally fell to pieces and, try as they might, patriotic leaders like Kamiakin and Looking Glass could not bring it back together. Only the spirits could do that.

The spirits did indeed come forward once again. An unprepossessing looking fellow, whose name was probably Waip-shwa, had a vision. Tradition holds that this young man died. While he was dead a mountain came to life and spoke to him, informing him that he was to be a great prophet and telling him to return to the world of the living. After several years of traveling, learning, and dreaming, Waip-shwa finally announced that Chief had commanded him to preach a new faith. The people immediately hailed him as a messenger from the chief spirit and renamed him Shmoqula, "The Prophet."[1]

Smohalla, as the whites called him, began preaching a message of hope for those Indians who could not live in the white man's world. He began with a newly revealed history of the world and its creation:

> Once the world was all water, and God lived alone; he was lonesome, he had no place to put his foot; so he scratched the sand up from the bottom, and made the land and he made rocks, and he made trees, and he made a man, and the man was winged and could go anywhere. The man was lonesome, and God made a woman. They ate fish from the water, and God made the deer and other animals, and he sent the man to hunt, and told the woman to cook the meat and to dress the skins. Many more men and women grew up, and they lived on the banks of the great river whose waters were full of salmon. The mountains contained much game, and there were buffalo on the plains. There were so many people that the stronger ones sometimes oppressed the weak and drove them from the best fisheries, which they claimed as their own. They fought, and nearly all were killed, and their bones are to be seen in the sand hills yet. God was very angry at

this, and he took away their wings and commanded that the lands and fisheries should be common to all who lived upon them. That they were never to be marked off or divided, but that the people should enjoy the fruits that God planted in the land and the animals that lived upon it, and the fishes in the water. God said he was the father, and the earth was the mother of mankind; that nature was the law; that the animals and fish and plants obeyed nature, and that man only was sinful. This is the old law.[2]

Then, Smohalla went on, new people had come:

First there were my people . . . God made them first. Then he made a Frenchman . . . , and then he made a priest . . . . A long time after that came "Boston man" . . . . And then "King George men" . . . . Bye and bye came "black man" . . . , and last he made a Chinaman with a tail. He is of no account, and has to work all the time. All these are new people; only the Indians are of the old stock.[3]

These newcomers had brought sinful ways with them, enticing the Indian people to abandon the old law. Sa'ghalee Tyee, the Great Chief Above, was angry at their apostasy and commanded the people through Smohalla to return to the old ways, pointing out that their present miserable condition in the presence of the whites was due to their having abandoned their own religion and violated the laws of nature and the precepts of their ancestors.[4]

Smohalla's message explained what had gone wrong. Chief's intentions had been misunderstood by the old Indian prophets. Mistakenly, the people had abandoned their simplicity and were now "suffering the penalty in all the misery that had come to them with the advent of the white-skin race that threatened to blot them out from the earth."[5] Because of this mistake, the world, instead of ending in the blissful return of the Earth Mother predicted by the previous prophets, had crumbled, leaving behind only a miasma of despair. "The whites have caused us great suffering," the Prophet said.

Dr Whitman many years ago made a long journey to the east to get a bottle of poisen for us. He was gone about a year, and after he came back strong and terrible diseases broke out among us.

The Indians killed Dr Whitman, but it was too late. He had un-corked his bottle and all the air was poisened. Before that there was little sickness among us, but since then many of us have died. I have had children and grandchildren, but they are all dead. My last grandchild, a young woman of 16, died last month. If only her infant could have lived. . . I labored hard to save them, but my medicine would not work as it used to.

We are now so few and weak that we can offer no resistance, and their preachers have persuaded them to let a few of us live, so as to claim credit with the Great Spirit for being generous and humane.[6]

To revive the old spirit power and to see to it that the whites did not get undeserved credit with the Great Spirit, Smohalla advocated to the survivors the complete abandonment of all of the new ways and a resumption of the old law. In an interview with the Prophet, Major J. W. MacMurray discovered that

Smohalla opposed anything that pertained to civilization, and had neither cattle, sheep, goats, pigs, nor chickens, and not a tree or vegetable was grown anywhere in his vicinage. Kowse (Peuceda-num cous), Kamas (Camassia esculenta), berries, fish, and the game of the mountains alone furnished food to his people, whom he advised to resist every advance of civilization as improper for a true Indian and in violation of the faith of their ancestors.[7]

"After awhile," Smohalla preached, "when God is ready, he will drive away all the people except the people who have obeyed the laws. Those who cut up the lands or sign papers for the lands will be defrauded of their rights, and will be punished by God's anger." Of the rest, the Prophet concluded, "All the dead men will come to life again; their spirits will come to their bodies again. We must wait here, in the homes of our fathers, and be ready to meet them in the bosom of our mother."[8] Here, then, was the new promise of salvation. The world of the earlier Prophets had indeed ended only in pain and suffering; but a new Indian world had come into existence and promised to end in the previously anticipated glory if the people remained true. What was more, the people need not do anything except wait and dream. "My young men shall never work," the Prophet pro-claimed. "Men who work can not dream, and wisdom comes to us in dreams . . . Each one must learn for himself the highest wisdom. It can not be taught."[9]

It is no surprise that the new faith tended to spread in direct proportion to the spread of the reservation system and the elimination of self-rule and self-determination. Possessed of a wisdom that the whites could not take away and the promise of a better life to come, those Indians who could not live in the white world could settle back to dream, rising only when the land to which the dead would return was threatened. The spirit power remained alive in this new Indian world, and the destructive power of the white invaders could not penetrate it. In this isolated realm the "dreamers" found the peace and safety that had prevailed under the old law.

Unlike the Plateau Indians' prophetic world, the whites' world survived the shock of the Whitman Massacre and the events that followed. Typical true believers, the missionaries, as contradictory evidence mounted, became even more entrenched in their beliefs.[10] In that rigid dualistic system, the Indian rejection of the white mission could only mean that the Plateau people had rejected God's offer of salvation and had joined forces with those who opposed both Protestantism and Americanism. As one born-again American said of the Plateau situation later in the century, "The rule is as fixed as the stars, that the sins of the fathers shall be visited upon the children unto the third and fourth generations of the men who hate God."[11] Spalding was especially disappointed and embittered and spent much of the rest of his life trying to prove that Whitman had been the victim of a Catholic and Indian conspiracy.[12]

Spalding remained in exile in the Willamette Valley until 1871, when he was appointed under U. S. Grant's peace policy as the superintendent of instruction for the Nez Perce.[13] In this role, he and his direct supervisor, Presbyterian layman John Monteith, along with a born-again military man, General Oliver Otis Howard, found themselves confronted with Smohalla's new vision and did their best to root it out. This led eventually to the infamous Nez Perce War of 1877 and the exile of Hin-mah-too-yah-lat-kekht (Chief Joseph) and others who were thought to be "dreamers."[14] With this irritation removed, the whites on the

Plateau continued to work toward their Manifest Destiny until the frontier simply passed them by.

The Plateau Indians, too, continued to work toward their destiny. In their case, this involved trying to find a spiritual system that would allow them to pull their shattered world together. Many religious movements have sprung up on the Plateau or have found their way there, but so far Smohalla's dream has not come to pass.[15] Still, there are many among the Plateau people who continue to dream of the time when the white world will end and the prophets of the white millennium will disappear. Then the people will again have the chance to live together with father sun and mother earth as was intended before the prophets met.

Notes

Introduction

1. The reader should be aware that there was a third cognitive world involved as well. Under the energetic leadership of Pierre Jean de Smet, European-trained Jesuits also entered the Plateau as missionaries. Like both their Protestant and Indian brethren, these priests partook of an ideological complex that colored their perception of the world around them. Though their presence and peculiar behavior contributed to the nature of Indian-white relations on the Plateau, this study gives them only brief attention. The dynamics of Indian-Catholic relations in the Plateau are so fascinating and complex that they warrent a similar synthesizing essay. Perhaps this study of the Protestant side may prompt one.

2. On the view of missionaries, see Clifton Jackson Phillips, *Protestant America and the Pagan World*; Robert F. Berkhofer, *Salvation and the Savage*; Clifford M. Drury, *Elkanah and Mary Walker*; idem, *Henry Harmon Spalding*; idem, *Marcus and Narcissa Whitman and the Opening of Old Oregon*; and idem, *Marcus Whitman, M.D.* For the Indians, see Lucellus V. McWhorter, *Yellow Wolf*; idem, *Hear Me, My Chiefs!*; Alvin M. Josephy, *The Nez Perce Indians and the Opening of the Northwest*; and

Deward E. Walker, Jr., *Mutual Crossutilization of Economic Resources in the Plateau* and idem, *Conflict and Schism in Nez Perce Acculturation.*

3. Fernand Braudel, "History and the Social Sciences: The *Longue Durée*," *Annales E.S.C.* 4 (1958): 725–753, reprinted in Braudel, *On History.*

4. Robert F. Berkhofer, "Paradigms for Interpreting the Past." For a more detailed discussion of Berkhofer's views, see his *A Behavioral Approach to Historical Analysis.* Braudel would, I think, agree with this assertion; see his discussion on *unconscious history* in "History and the Social Sciences," 39.

5. James Axtell, "Ethnohistory: An Historian's Viewpoint," in Axtell, *The European and the Indian,* 5. A cross-section of views on ethnohistory presented by such writers as Wilcomb Washburn, Nancy Oestreich Lurie, and David A. Baerreis may be found in *Ethnohistory* 8 (1961): 12–92. See also Calvin Martin, "Ethnohistory."

6. Axtell, "Ethnohistory," 8.

7. Calvin Martin, *Keepers of the Game,* 20.

8. Keith Thomas, *Religion and the Decline of Magic.* It is interesting to note that historians specializing in early modern studies are beginning to turn toward a more ethnohistorical approach, as evidenced by Peter Burke's current research into the psychosocial effects of literacy in Renaissance Italy.

9. This being said, I must confess that the discussion to come includes some generalizing of Plateau cultural traits. Plateau cultures, though not identical, were similar enough to consititute a single culture area. Where the subcultures disagreed, I try to note the exceptions. Protestant America was not a unitary entity, either, but consisted of many different, and often warring, factions. As with the Indian groups, I acknowledge, but do not emphasize in the text, the differences between groups such as Methodists, Congregationalists, and Presbyterians.

10. Martin, *Keepers of the Game,* 6.

11. Reuben Gold Thwaites, ed., *Original Journals of the Lewis and Clark Expedition* 3:105; Gen. Nelson A. Miles, quoted in Merrill Beal, *"I Will Fight No More Forever,"* 5; McWhorter, *Hear Me, My Chiefs!* 2.

12. James Penny Boyd, "The Nez Perce War," in his *Recent Indian Wars, under the Lead of Sitting Bull and Other Chiefs*; Beal, *"I Will Fight No More Forever"*; Robert I. Burns, *The Jesuits and the Indian Wars of the Northwest.*

13. Oliver Otis Howard, *Nez Perce Joseph,* 18.

14. See Josephy, *Nez Perce Indians.*
15. Wilbur R. Jacobs, *Dispossessing the American Indian,* 108.

Chapter 1. The Plateau World

1. Verne F. Ray, *The Sanpoil and Nespelem,* 12; idem, *Cultural Relations in the Plateau of Northwestern America,* 1; Henry P. Hansen, "Postglacial Forest Secession, Climate, and Chronology in the Pacific Northwest," 47–70.
2. Ray, *Sanpoil and Nespelem,* 26.
3. Luther S. Cressman, *Prehistory of the Far West,* 73; Arnoud Stryd and Rachel Smith, eds., *Aboriginal Man and Environments on the Plateau of Northwest America,* 9; Earl H. Swanson, Jr., "Early Cultures in Northwestern America," 81; Charles E. Bordon, "Notes and News"; Frank C. Leonhardy and David G. Rice, "A Proposed Culture Typology for the Lower Snake River Region, Southeastern Washington," 1; Ray, *Cultural Relations,* 145.
4. Ray, *Cultural Relations,* 147–149; Carl F. Voegelin and Florence M. Voegelin, *Map of North American Indian Languages;* idem, "Languages of the World: Native American Fascicle One" and "Native American Fascicle Two."
5. The leading monograph on this subject is Angelo Anastasio, "The Southern Plateau," the whole thrust of which is essentially this point. See also Bill B. Brunton, "Ceremonial Integration in the Plateau of Northwestern America," 12–13 and Ray, *Cultural Relations,* 149, 145.
6. Verne F. Ray, *Ethnohistory of the Joseph Band of Nez Perce Indians,* 179; idem, *Cultural Relations,* 10.
7. Ray, *Sanpoil and Nespelem,* 109–111; Walker, *Conflict and Schism,* 9–13, 16–17; Anastasio, "Southern Plateau," 189–190.
8. Allen P. Slickpoo, *Noon nee-me-poo,* 52; Ray, *Cultural Relations,* 12. I use the term tribe here as a literary convention despite Angelo Anastasio's suggestion (Anastasio to C. L. Miller, 29 June 1983) that the word group would be more accurate.
9. Angelo Anastasio, *Ethnohistory of the Spokan Indians,* 170.
10. Anastasio, "Southern Plateau," 148–154.
11. Ibid., 156.
12. Ibid., 137–139; Stuart A. Chalfant, *Aboriginal Territory of the Nez Perce Indians,* 133–134.

13. Ray, *Sanpoil and Nespelem*, 27; Herbert J. Spinden, *The Nez Perce Indians*, 203–204; Chalfant, *Aboriginal Territory*, 135.

14. Spinden, *Nez Perce Indians*, 204–208; Ray, *Sanpoil and Nespelem*, 28; Chalfant, *Aboriginal Territory*, 135.

15. Spinden, *Nez Perce Indians*, 200, 202–203, 206, 211; Livingston Farrand, "Notes on the Nez Perce Indians," 245; James A. Teit, *The Salishan Tribes of the Western Plateaus*, 96; Ray, *Sanpoil and Nespelem*, 28; Slickpoo, *Noon nee-me-poo*, 35; Chalfant, *Aboriginal Territory*, 136–137.

16. Spinden, *Nez Perce Indians*, 206.

17. Periodic famines were not uncommon in the Pacific Northwest but were infrequent enough that no special preparations were made for them; see Wayne Suttles, "Coping with Abundance," 58–61. Famine is graphically illustrated in Plateau Indian folklore; see "Greedy Coyote, His Friend the Fox, and Woodtick," in Allen P. Slickpoo, *Nu Mee poom tit wah tit*, 167–169.

18. Slickpoo, *Nu Mee poom tit wah tit*, xv–xvi.

19. Ibid.

20. Spinden, *Nez Perce Indians*, 260.

21. Spirit experiences were not identical among all Plateau groups. Generally speaking, there were two basic patterns to spirit quests among the Columbia Plateau dwellers: the Sanpoil and the Kutenai styles. The biggest difference between the two patterns was that, in the former, the spirit experience was forgotten until the person attained maturity, whereas in the latter, the experience was not forgotten and was reported immediately. A third, the Carrier style, also differed in some respects not important here. The general thrust of spirit life was otherwise very similar and can be discussed without too much attention to individual differences. For further information on the guardian spirit complex, see Ruth F. Benedict, *The Concept of the Guardian Spirit in North America*, 62–63. More specific data on the complex as practiced on the Plateau may be found in Ray, *Cultural Relations*, 68–69, 72, 79; Slickpoo, *Nu Mee poom tit wah tit*, 201–202; McWhorter, *Yellow Wolf*, 296; Kate McBeth, *Nez Perces since Lewis and Clark*, 259–260; Farrand, "Notes on the Nez Perce," 245; and Deward E. Walker, Jr., "A Nez Perce Ethnographic Observation of Archaeological Significance," 437.

22. Slickpoo, *Nu Mee poom tit wah tit*, 201–202; Ray, *Cultural Relations*, 68, 77.

23. Spinden, *Nez Perce Indians*, 249.

24. McWhorter, *Yellow Wolf*, 299.

25. Ray, *Cultural Relations*, 95–100.

26. Spinden, *Nez Perce Indians*, 247–248; Walker, "Nez Perce Ethnographic Observation," 437.

27. Spinden, *Nez Perce Indians*, 262; Ray, *Cultural Relations*, 103–104; Slickpoo, *Noon nee-me-poo*, 61.

28. Ray, *Sanpoil and Nespelem*, 196, 199–200.

29. Ray, *Cultural Relations*, 103.

30. See Walker, *Mutual Crossutilization*.

31. Sue Whalen, "The Nez Perces' Relationship to Their Land," 30–32.

32. Jamake Highwater, *The Primal Mind: Vision and Reality in Indian America*, 56, 170–173; Claude Levi-Strauss, *The Savage Mind*. Psychological research lends credence to this interpretation of Indian identity. See A. R. Luria, *Cognitive Development*, 145–159. For a discussion of this identity issue in a theraputic context see Carolyn Attneave, "American Indians and Alaska Native Families: Emigrants in their Own Homeland," 66–69.

33. Marian W. Smith, "The War Complex of the Plains Indians," 434.

34. Highwater, *Primal Mind*, 174; Slickpoo, *Noon nee-me-poo*, 57–58; Walker, *Conflict and Schism*, 23–25.

35. Walker, *Conflict and Schism*, 29–30.

36. "A society whose members are united by the fact that they think in the same way in regard to the sacred world and its relations with the profane world, and by the fact that they translate these common ideas into common practices, is what is called a church." Emile Durkheim, *Elementary Forms of Religious Life*, 44.

Chapter 2. The Eighteenth-Century Crisis

1. Ellsworth Huntington, *The Climatic Factor as Illustrated in Arid America*, 66; David A. Baerreis and Reid A. Bryson, "Climatic Episodes and the Dating of the Mississippian Culture," 204, 216–217; Robert Claiborne, *Climate, Man, and History*, 225; H. H. Lamb, *Climate* 2:449.

2. Emmanuel Le Roy Ladurie, *Times of Feast, Times of Famine*, 26.

3. Huntington, *The Climatic Factor*, 323 (table G.); Le Roy Ladurie, *Time of Feast*, 31–34.

4. H. H. Lamb, *Climate* 2:36.

5. Harold C. Fritts, G. Robert Lofgren, and Geoffrey A. Gordon,

"Past Climate Reconstruction from Tree Rings," 791–792. This entire number (4) of the *Journal of Interdisciplinary History* is devoted to discussions of climate and history with an emphasis on the Little Ice Age.

6. Thompson Webb III, "The Reconstruction of Climatic Sequences from Botanical Data," 759, 766.

7. Leonhardy and Rice, "Proposed Culture Typology," 20.

8. Frederick Alexander Davidson, *The Effect of Floods on the Upstream Migration of the Salmon in the Columbia River*, 19.

9. Baerreis and Bryson, "Climatic Episodes," 217.

10. There may, in fact, be some correlation between the declining weather conditions and European expansion into the Americas. Theodore K. Rabb has suggested that the Little Ice Age may have been influential in bringing on the seventeenth-century crisis in Europe and this, in turn, opened the way for the rise of overseas empires. See his *The Struggle for Stability in Early Modern Europe*, 85–89.

11. My use of the word "crisis" in this chapter corresponds with Rabb's definition relating to the "general crisis" in Europe during the seventeenth century. For a complete discussion, see his, *Struggle for Stability*, 29–34.

12. Slickpoo, *Noon nee-me-poo*, 31; Herbert J. Spinden, "Nez Perce Tales," 158; Francis Haines, "The Northward Spread of Horses among the Plains Indians," 434, 431.

13. Baerreis and Bryson, "Climatic Episodes," 217; James B. Griffin, "Some Correlations of Climatic and Cultural Change in Eastern North American Prehistory," 712; Reid A. Bryson, David A. Baerreis, and Wayne M. Wendland, "The Character of Late-glacial and Post-glacial Climatic Change," 64–65; H. H. Lamb, *Climate* 2:449; Waldo Wedel, "Culture Sequence in the Central Great Plains," 346; idem, "Environment and Native Subsistence Economies in the Central Great Plains," 19.

14. George Hyde, *Indians of the High Plains*, 137; Sydney M. Lamb, "Linguistic Prehistory in the Great Basin," 98–99; Dimitri Boris Shimkin, "Shoshoni-Commanche Origins and Migrations," 20; Haines, "Northward Spread of Horses."

15. Thwaites, *Original Journals* 4:73; Teit, *Salishan Tribes*, 352.

16. Chalfant, *Aboriginal Territory*, 139.

17. Spinden, *Nez Perce Indians*, 206; Slickpoo, *Noon nee-me-poo*, 35.

18. Reuben Gold Thwaites, ed., *The Jesuit Relations and Allied Documents* 50:307, 279; 51:21, 47, 63, 223; Wedel, "Culture Sequence," 326; Hyde, *Indians of the High Plains*, 77–78, 141, 186; Frank R. Secoy,

Changing Military Patterns on the Great Plains, 33; Oscar Lewis, *Effects of White Contact upon Blackfoot Culture with Special Reference to the Role of the Fur Trade*, 10.

19. Carling Malouf and A. Arline Malouf, "The Effects of Spanish Slavery on the Indians of the Intermountain West," 426–435; Secoy, *Changing Military Patterns*, 38; Hyde, *Indians of the High Plains*, 145.

20. Secoy, *Changing Military Patterns*, 38, 47; Hyde, *Indians of the High Plains*, 136–137; L. J. Burpee, ed., "York Fort to Blackfeet Country," 335, 338.

21. Julian Steward, *Basin-Plateau Aboriginal Sociopolitical Groups*, 208. The use of the term Snake follows Steward's observation that as a result of their early acquisition of the horse and "comparatively high degree of political solidarity," the Fort Hall Shoshoni should be distinguished from the more friendly Shoshoneans of Western Idaho. Since, as he continues, "Most often horse Shoshoni were called Snake and foot Shoshoni were Diggers, Shoshokoes or Shoshonee" (198–199), the word *Snake* is perhaps most descriptive of the Fort Hall people. For additional information on the Snake-Bannock connection, see Shimkin, "Shoshoni-Commanche Origins and Migrations," 20; Robert F. Murphy and Yolanda Murphy, *Shoshone-Bannock Subsistence and Society*; Brigham D. Madsen, *The Bannock of Idaho*; and idem, *The Lemhi*.

22. Bernard Mishkin, *Rank and Warfare among the Plains Indians*, 57; Secoy, *Changing Military Patterns*, 58; Teit, *Salishan Tribes*, 126, 316; Hyde, *Indians of the High Plains*, 191; Murphy and Murphy, *Shoshone-Bannock Subsistence and Society*, 295.

23. Secoy, *Changing Military Patterns*, 58.

24. Ibid., 47.

25. Alexander Henry, *Travels and Adventures in Canada and the Indian Territories between the Years 1760 and 1776*, 303–304.

26. Secoy, *Changing Military Patterns*, 51–52; O. Lewis, *Effects of White Contact*, 36; George Bird Grinnell, "Early Blackfoot History," 164; John C. Ewers, *The Horse in Blackfoot Indian Culture, with Comparative Material from Other Western Tribes*, 13.

27. E. E. Rich, ed., *Cumberland House Journals and Inland Journal*, 1:168; Ewers, *Horse in Blackfoot Culture*, 175; Abraham Phineas Nasatir, ed., *Before Lewis and Clark*, 332; Charles Mackenzie, "The Missouri Indians," 346.

28. Ewers, *Horse in Blackfoot Culture*, 176. The general preference for children and females as captives and slaves is discussed in Malouf and Malouf, "Effects of Spanish Slavery," 434.

29. Elliott Coues, ed., *New Light on the Early History of the Northwest*, 526.

30. Teit, *Salishan Tribes*, 303, 317–318. According to Harry H. Turney-High, the Tuna'xe survived but ceased to be an independent social group. The survivors fled and joined the Western Kutenai; see Turney-High, *Ethnography of the Kutenai*, 13. An account of the Flathead withdrawal told by an informant named Faro may be found in Warren Angus Ferris, *Life in the Rocky Mountains*, 91.

31. See E. E. Rich, *The Fur Trade and the Northwest to 1857*.

32. Mackenzie, "Missouri Indians," 331.

33. Rich, *Fur Trade and the Northwest*, 215–216.

34. W. F. Wentzel, "Letters to the Hon. Roderick McKenzie," 106.

35. Mackenzie, "Missouri Indians," 331.

36. Arthur S. Morton, ed., *The Journal of Duncan M'Gillivray of the Northwest Company at Fort George on the Saskatchewan*, 52.

37. Ibid., 55.

38. Ibid., 31, 47.

39. Ibid., 56.

40. Teit, *Salishan Tribes*, 318; Ewers, *Horse in Blackfoot Culture*, 7.

41. Henry F. Dobyns, "Estimating Aboriginal American Populations," 411–412. See also Alfred W. Crosby, *The Columbian Exchange* and William H. McNeill, *Plagues and Peoples*.

42. Rich, ed., *Cumberland House Journals and Inland Journal* 1:298.

43. Ibid., 238–298.

44. Anastasio, "Southern Plateau," 209; Teit, *Salishan Tribes*, 315.

45. A. J. Allen, *Ten Years in Oregon*, 317. While I do not cite White's figure as a statement of fact concerning prehistoric Indian populations in the Pacific Northwest, it is significant that, as a participant in the historical events of the period and as a witness to Indian disease and depopulation, White believed the decline to be this radical. Although I would prefer to not get involved in the highly technical and politically thorny question of Indian demography, I should point out that, based on figures derived from Sherburne Cook, Dobyns has estimated that populations among northwestern riverine Indians declined by 75 percent during the 1830–1833 epidemic alone; see Dobyns, "Estimating Aboriginal American Populations," 410–411 and also H. C. Taylor and L. L. Hoaglin, Jr., "The 'Intermittent Fever' Epidemic of the 1830's on the Lower Columbia River." It is also worth noting that figures cited by William Cronon (*Changes In the Land*, 87) concerning New England population decline for the contact period agree very closely with White's figure for the Pacific Northwest during its initial contact period.

Chapter 3. The Plateau Prophecy

1. Slickpoo, *Noon nee-me-poo*, 52; Deward E. Walker, Jr., *American Indians of Idaho*, 71–72; Ray, *Cultural Relations*, 13–14; Steward, *Basin-Plateau Aboriginal Sociopolitical Groups*, 232.

2. Teit, *Salishan Tribes*, 156.

3. Allen, *Ten Years in Oregon*, 317.

4. Ray, *Cultural Relations*, 10; Chalfant, *Aboriginal Territory*, 5; Alexander Ross, *Fur Hunters of the Far West*, 222.

5. Mishkin, *Rank and Warfare among the Plains Indians*, 14n; Spinden, *Nez Perce Indians*, 271.

6. Charles Wilkes, *Narrative of the United States Exploring Expedition during the years 1838, 1839, 1840, 1841 and 1842* 4:447; John Dunn, *History of the Oregon Territory and the British American Fur Trade*, 208; Anastasio, *Ethnohistory of the Spokan Indians*, 148.

7. Dunn, *Oregon Territory*, 208; Ray, *Cultural Relations*, 29.

8. Walker, *Mutual Crossutilization*, 14, 8.

9. Slickpoo, *Noon nee-me-poo*, 24.

10. Verne F. Ray, "The Columbia Indian Confederacy;" Anastasio, "Southern Plateau," 150. Ross noted that "the Cayouses, the Nez Perce, and other warlike tribes assemble every spring in the Eyakemas [Yakima Valley] . . . It is, therefore the great national rendezvous, where thousands meet"; Ross, *Fur Hunters of the Far West*, 5. One such camp consisted of Flathead, Pend d'Oreille, Kutenai, Nez Perce, and Spokan. T. C. Elliott, ed., "Journal of Alexander Ross," 386. Such a congregation certainly does not reflect mounting national tensions.

11. Ray, "Columbia Indian Confederacy," 773.

12. My interpretation of the dynamic pressures confronting the Plateau people and their religious response is contested by many. The best discussion of the controversy surrounding this issue is Deward E. Walker, Jr., "New Light on the Prophet Dance Controversy."

13. Anthony F. C. Wallace, "Revitalization Movements," 266.

14. Ibid., 269, 267.

15. Anthony F. C. Wallace, *The Death and Rebirth of the Seneca*, 251–252.

16. Some anthropological theorists maintain that a revitalization movement can take place only when a culture is exposed to strong deculturating forces through contact with another radically different (or, perhaps, "superior") culture; see Ralph Linton, "Nativistic Movements," and Robert Redfield, Ralph Linton, and Melville J. Herskovits, "Memorandum for the Study of Acculturation." For a dissenting and

more flexible view, see Edward Norbeck, *Religion in Primitive Society*, 263–264. In line with Walker's and David Chance's opinions, it would appear that white deculturating forces were influential in bringing on this revitalization, although natural forces were also at work; see Walker, "Prophet Dance Controversy," 247 and David H. Chance, *Influences of the Hudson's Bay Company on the Native Cultures of the Colvile District*, 71–72.

17. Wilkes, *Narrative* 4:439.

18. Teit, *Salishan Tribes*, 291.

19. Ray, *Sanpoil and Nespelem*, 189.

20. Wilkes, *Narrative* 4:439; Teit, *Salishan Tribes*, 201; Ray, *Sanpoil and Nespelem*, 108; Leslie Spier, *The Prophet Dance of the Northwest and Its Derivatives*, 8; Wayne Suttles, "The Plateau Prophet Dance among the Coast Salish," 392.

21. Spinden, *Nez Perce Indians*, 268; see also R. L. Packard, "Notes on the Mythology and Religion of the Nez Perce."

22. Franz Boas, ed., *Folk-Tales of Salishan and Sahaptin Tribes*, 83.

23. Spier, *Prophet Dance*, 5.

24. Leslie Spier, ed., *The Sinkaietk or Southern Okanagon of Washington*, 174–175.

25. Ibid.

26. Secoy, *Changing Military Patterns*, 58; Thwaites, *Original Journals* 5:24; McWhorter, *Hear Me, My Chiefs!* 12–13.

27. Wilkes, *Narrative* 4:439.

28. Ibid.; Spier, *Prophet Dance*, 55–63; McWhorter, *Hear Me, My Chiefs!* 17–18.

29. Thwaites, *Original Journals* 3:77, 84–86; McWhorter, *Hear Me, My Chiefs!* 16.

30. Thwaites, *Original Journals* 5:24.

31. Ibid., 14–15, 18–19.

32. Ibid., 21–22.

33. Ibid., 299–301.

34. Ibid., 24.

35. Ibid., 24, 105.

36. Ibid., 23.

37. Ibid., 113.

38. Ibid., 158, 42.

39. Ibid., 222–223. The wounded Indian later died of his injuries. For addition details, see T. Biddle to Col. H. Atkinson, 29 October 1819, *American State Papers: Indian Affairs* 2:202.

40. "Statement of Appropriations and Expenditures on Account of Trading-houses with the Indian Tribes, from the 4th March, 1789 to the 31st December, 1819," *American State Papers: Indian Affairs* 2:221; Hiram M. Chittenden, *The American Fur Trade of the Far West*, 17n.

41. McWhorter, *Hear Me, My Chiefs!* 13–15. At the conclusion of this war, the Plateau people and the Snake oscillated between amity and bellicosity until the power of both was broken by war with the whites.

42. T. Biddle to Col. H. Atkinson, 29 October 1819, *American State Papers: Indian Affairs* 2:201–202; Richard Glover, ed., *David Thompson's Narrative*, 273, 302, 316; H. M. Brackenridge, *Views of Louisiana*, 92; Chittenden, *American Fur Trade*, 706.

43. Glover, *David Thompson's Narrative*, 373.

44. Spier, *Prophet Dance*, 19.

Chapter 4. The Prophecy Unfolds

1. David Thompson, Journals, 1806–1812 (hereafter cited as David Thompson Journals). See the entries for July 1811 for descriptions of the dances and the frequency of their performance.

2. David Thompson Journals, 3 July 1811.

3. See Ray, *Sanpoil and Nespelem*, 189; Suttles, "Plateau Prophet Dance"; and Spier, *Prophet Dance*.

4. Spier, *Prophet Dance*, 19.

5. Mine is, quite frankly, a spiritualistic reading of the events and disagrees to some extent with Walker's interpretation, which stresses the "cargo cult" angle to the Indians' appeal for white assistance; see Walker, "Prophet Dance Controversy," 250–252. Given the all pervasive nature of spirit life among Plateau people, I find a totally materialistic interpretation unconvincing, but I acknowledge that part of the appeal of the "white man's God" would surely have been the skills and materials that this novel spirit granted those who entered into a relationship with it.

6. For an overview of the fur trade in the area, see Rich, *Fur Trade and the Northwest*. See also Josephy, *Nez Perce Indians*, 40–78.

7. Lawrence B. Palladino, *Indian and White in the Northwest*, 8–9.

8. Ibid.

9. Spier, *Prophet Dance*, 31.

10. Suttles, "Plateau Prophet Dance."

11. Spier, *Prophet Dance*, 35.

12. Palladino, *Indian and White in the Northwest*, 9.

13. E. E. Rich, *The History of the Hudson's Bay Company*, 401, 471–476, 573, 620.

14. Ibid., 528.

15. Rich, *Fur Trade and the Northwest*, 255–256.

16. Reverend David T. Jones, quoted in J. Orin Oliphant, "George Simpson and the Oregon Missions," 234.

17. Slickpoo, *Noon nee-me-poo*, 70.

18. Frederick Merk, ed., *Fur Trade and Empire*, 54.

19. Ibid., 108.

20. Ibid., 106.

21. Reverend David Jones to the Church Mission Society, quoted in Oliphant, "Simpson and the Oregon Missions," 234.

22. Ibid., 239.

23. Merk, *Fur Trade and Empire*, 135, 138.

24. Clifford M. Drury, "Oregon Indians in the Red River School," 54.

25. Oliphant, "Simpson and the Oregon Missions," 243.

26. David Douglas, *Journal Kept by David Douglas During His Travels in North America*, 280.

27. Oliphant, "Simpson and the Oregon Missions," 243.

28. William S. Lewis, "The Case of Spokane Garry," 14.

29. Spier, *Prophet Dance*, 37.

30. Oliphant, "Simpson and the Oregon Missions," 243.

31. Ibid., 241.

32. Harrison C. Dale, ed., *The Ashley-Smith Explorations and the Discovery of a Central Route to the Pacific*, 109; Chittenden, *American Fur Trade*, 281; Ferris, *Life in the Rocky Mountains*, xci–cv.

33. Ferris, *Life in the Rocky Mountains*, 96.

34. Clifford M. Drury, *Chief Lawyer of the Nez Perce*, 26; Asa B. Smith to David Greene, 27 August 1839, quoted in ibid., 29.

35. Drury, *Chief Lawyer*, 30.

36. Nez Perce ambivalence about the Hudson's Bay Company is revealed by most of the principals involved in the fur trade. For example, throughout the late 1820s Peter Skene Ogden found it increasingly difficult to secure horses and provisions from the Nez Perce, whereas the American traders had little or no difficulty; see Glyndwr Williams, ed., *Peter Skene Ogden's Snake Country Journals*, 177n, 31. For a more complete discussion, see Josephy, *Nez Perce Indians*, 62–70.

37. Josephy, *Nez Perce Indians*, 80; Drury, *Chief Lawyer*, 26, 30.

38. Ferris, *Life in the Rocky Mountains*, 87.

39. Marcus Whitman, "Journal and Report by Dr. Marcus Whitman of His Tour of Exploration with Rev. Samuel Parker in 1825 beyond the Rocky Mountains," 256.

40. G. P. Disoway to the Editor, 1 March 1833, *Christian Advocate and Journal and Zion's Herald* 7 (1833): 105.

41. William Walker to G. P. Disoway, 19 January 1833, in *Christian Advocate and Journal and Zion's Herald* 7 (1833): 105.

42. Ibid.

43. Francis Haines (in "The Nez Perce Delegation to St. Louis in 1831," 78) summarized the evidence against such a meeting: "That Walker did not see the famous delegation is proved by these items,

"Walker arrived in St. Louis in the fall (probably November) of 1832. The two surviving Indians had left St. Louis March 26, 1832.

"Walker's description could not possibly apply to these Indians or any other Indians known to be in St. Louis at the time. He apparently talked to someone who had seen north coast Indians but who had not seen the delegation.

"Had Walker met the Indians, he probably would not have called them all chiefs, and he would have known that Clark did not speak Nez Perce as fluently as Walker describes."

Drury disputes this, claiming that Haines does not present sufficient evidence to negate Walker's testimony. Drury, however, presents no evidence to support his position, and the overwhelmingly negative nature of the other evidence leads to the suspicion that Haines is correct; see Drury, "The Nez Perce Delegation of 1831," 283–284. As for the description of the Indians, one man in St. Louis had definitely seen north coast Indians: William Clark. If, as Haines insists, Walker was in St. Louis a year after the Flathead delegation, then it could be that he heard the whole story, including the description, from Clark. What the superintendent's motivation would have been for so freely embroidering upon the story can only be conjectured.

44. Bishop Joseph Rosati to *l'Association de la Propagation de la Foi*, 31 (December 1831), in Archer B. Hulbert, ed., *The Charles B. Voorhis Series of Overland to the Pacific* 5:87–88.

45. Ibid. 5:88; Disoway to the Editor, 1 March 1833.
46. Disoway to the Editor, 1 March 1833.

Chapter 5. The White Prophecy

1. [Calvin Colton] A Protestant, *Protestant Jesuitism*, 114.
2. U. S. Department of the Census, *Historical Statistics of the United States*, 33, 8.
3. George Rogers Taylor, *The Transportation Revolution*, 158, 136.
4. Ibid., 21, 50. Edward Pessen estimates that the dollar of 1840 was worth between 5 and 5½ 1970 dollars; Pessen "The Egalitarian Myth and the American Social Reality," 997.
5. Douglass C. North, *The Economic Growth of the United States, 1790–1860*, 25, 181.
6. Thomas Jefferson to John Adams, 28 October 1813 in Thomas Jefferson, *The Writings of Thomas Jefferson* 14:396.
7. Thomas Jefferson, *Notes on the State of Virginia*, 148–149.
8. See Chilton Williamson, *American Suffrage from Property to Democracy*. See also Glyndon G. Van Deusen, *The Jacksonian Era*, 10–11.
9. Perry Miller, *The Life of the Mind in America*, 6–7. See also William W. Sweet, *Revivalism in America*; idem, *Religion in the Development of American Culture*; Timothy L. Smith, *Revivalism and Social Reform in Mid-nineteenth Century America*; Sidney E. Mead, *The Lively Experiment: The Shaping of Christianity in America*; George M. Marsden, *The Evangelical Mind and the New School Presbyterian Experience*; James Ward Smith and A. L. Jamison, *The Shaping of American Religion*; and Whitney R. Cross, *The Burned Over District*.
10. Sweet, *Religion*, 200; T. L. Smith, *Revivalism and Social Reform*, 104.
11. William W. Sweet, "Protestantism and Democracy," in *American Culture and Religion*, 37; Sweet, *Religion*, 210.
12. Miller, *Life of the Mind*, 20. The nature of this religious movement suggests that, like the Plateau, America underwent a cultural revitalization. Certainly the nation was being subjected to enormous stress that could have produced mazeway restructuring. This aspect of American cultural and religious history needs further research.
13. T. L. Smith, *Revivalism and Social Reform*, 108; Wallace, "Revitalization Movements," 268; Donald C. Mathews, "The Second Great Awakening as an Organizing Process," 39.

14. Quoted in Marsden, *Evangelical Mind*, 17.

15. On millennialism, see Ernest R. Sandeen, *The Roots of Fundamentalism*; see also Ernest Lee Tuveson, *Redeemer Nation*.

16. Lyman Beecher, *A Plea For The West*, 10.

17. Thomas Hart Benton, "Address before Congress, January 3, 1825," in U. S. Congress, *Abridgment of Debates of Congress from 1789 to 1856* 8:197.

18. Alexander McLeod, *A Scriptural View of the Character, Causes, and Ends of the Present War*, 220.

19. Ray Allen Billington, *The Protestant Crusade*.

20. Samuel F. B. Morse, *Imminent Dangers to the Free Institutions of the United States through Foreign Immigration and the Present State of the Naturalization Laws*, 8.

21. Samuel F. B. Morse, *The Foreign Conspiracy against the Liberties of the United States*, 19, 21–22

22. Beecher, *Plea For The West*, 54.

23. Ibid., 56.

24. John Ferling, "The American Revolution and American Security," 505.

25. T. S. Jessup, U.S. quartermaster general, to Senator John Floyd, 6 April 1824, 18th Cong., 1st. sess. Senate Document 56.

26. John C. Calhoun, secretary of war, to House Committee on Military Affairs, 29 December 1829, *American State Papers: Military Affairs* 2:33–34; Joshua Pilcher to J. H. Eaton, secretary of war, undated, and Jedediah S. Smith, David E. Jackson, and William L. Sublette to J. H. Eaton, secretary of war, 29 October 1830, Senate Document 39, 21st Cong., 2d. sess.; Select Committee on the Bill to Authorize the President to Occupy the Oregon Territory, *Report*, 25th Cong., 2d. sess.

27. Smith, Jackson, and Sublette to Eaton, 29 October 1830, Senate Document 39, 21st Cong., 2d. sess.

28. Morse, *Foreign Conspiracy*, 101, 124.

29. G. Gordon Brown, "Missionaries and Cultural Diffusion," 214, 217; Albert K. Weinberg, *Manifest Destiny*, 3.

30. Phillips, *Protestant America*, 242.

31. U. S. Congress, *Annals of Congress*, 16th Cong., 2d. sess. 37:958–959; ibid., 17th Cong., 2d. sess. 40:396.

32. Ibid., 17th Cong., 2d. sess. 40:422–424, 591–601; Reginald Horsman, *Race and Manifest Destiny*, 81–97.

33. U. S. Congress, *Register of Debates in Congress* 1:711–713.

34. Hall Jackson Kelley, "To a Member of Congress, on the Settlement of the Oregon Country, No. 9." See also Fred W. Powell, "Hall

Jackson Kelley, Prophet of Oregon," and idem, ed., *Hall Jackson Kelley on Oregon.*

35. Hall Jackson Kelley, "To a Member of Congress, on the Settlement of the Oregon Country, No. 8."

36. S. Adams, "Account of the North-West Coast: Read before the 'Society of Inquiry on Missions' in the Theological Seminary, Andover. July 23, 1822," *Boston Recorder* 7 (1822): 125, 128.

37. Ibid., 128.

38. "A Plymouth Colony for Oregon, Address of the Prudential Committee of the American Board of Commissioners for Foreign Missions," *Missionary Herald* 23 (1827): 396–397. The view of Manifest Destiny and mission presented here departs somewhat from that to be found in most of the literature on the other subject. Frederick Merk (*Manifest Destiny and Mission in American History*) was quite correct to criticize Weinberg's earlier assertion that Manifest Destiny was simply nationalism gone mad. At the same time, however, Merk's discussion of early-nineteenth-century mission as a genuine expression of altruism standing in contrast to a cynical post-1844 Manifest Destiny simply does not hold up. The same problem arises in Reginald Horsman's recent work *Race and Manifest Destiny*, in which one sees a process similar to (though much more sophisticated than) that described by Merk. According to Horsman the motivating force is emergent "racialism" and the pivotal date is 1830. Although all of these arguments have merit, it must be pointed out that altruism may be found in expansionistic appeals after 1830 (or 1844) and that cynicism may be detected before these pivotal dates. This relatively early attempt on the part of the ABCFM serves as an excellent illustration of the points raised by Mathews ("Second Great Awakening") and T. Scott Miyakawa (*Protestants and Pioneers*) concerning the social-control aspects of the Second Great Awakening. This, taken in conjunction with Clifford Griffin's *Their Brothers' Keepers* and Lois Banner's "Religious Benevolence as Social Control," indicates that, even in the most humanitarian organizations, cynicism and altruism worked hand-in-hand. Shielded from dissonance by the shimmering mantle of truly unselfish *mission*, nineteenth-century evangelicals were able to go about the business of Manifest Destiny undisturbed.

39. "A Plymouth Colony for Oregon," 396–397.

40. J. S. Green, "Extracts from the Report of an Exploring Tour on the North-West Coast of North America in 1829," *Missionary Herald* 27 (1831): 33–39, 75–77, 105–107.

41. Report of the Standing Committee on Oregon Missions, 20 January 1830, printed in Hulbert, *Overland* 5:81–82.

42. General Conference of the Methodist Episcopal Church, Committee on Missions, "Report," *New England Christian Herald*, 17 June 1832, reprinted in Hulbert, *Overland* 5:101.

43. "Review of Ross Cox's *Adventures on the Columbia River*," *Methodist Magazine and Quarterly Review* 14 (N.S. 3) (1832): 274–313.

44. Ibid., 312.

45. Hall Jackson Kelley, "To a Member of Congress, on the Settlement of the Oregon Country, No. 1."

46. Ibid., "No. 8."

Chapter 6. The Prophets Meet

1. Robert Moulton Gatke, ed., "A Document of Mission History," 72–73.

2. A. M'Allister to the Editor, 17 April 1833, *Christian Advocate and Journal and Zion's Herald* 7 (1833): 146.

3. Gatke, "Document of Mission History," 73–74.

4. Jason Lee, "The Diary of Jason Lee," 116–119, 261, 399.

5. Rev. Samuel Parker to the secretaries, American Board of Commissioners for Foreign Missions, 10 April 1833. Papers of the ABCFM: 6, vol. 11, entry 32 (hereafter cited as ABC).

6. Parker to David Greene, 27 May 1834. ABC:18.3.1, vol. 9, entry 178.

7. Parker to Greene, 25 December 1834. ABC:18.3.1, vol. 9, entry 180.

8. Greene to Parker, 7 January 1835. ABC:1.2.1, vol. 2, p. 142. A note to this effect signed by B. B. Wisner is appended to Marcus Whitman to B. B. Wisner, 27 June 1834, American Board of Commissioners for Foreign Missions, "Correspondence Relating to Applications of Missionaries to Oregon Territory," (hereafter cited as ABCFM, "Correspondence").

9. Parker to Greene, 9 June 1835. ABC:18.3.1, vol. 9, entry 186.

10. Rev. Samuel Parker, *Journal of an Exploring Tour Beyond the Rocky Mountains; Under the direction of the ABCFM, performed in the years 1835, '36, and '37*, 76–77.

11. Ibid., 78.

12. Whitman to Greene, 7 November 1835, ABCFM, "Correspondence."

13. Greene to Whitman, 6 January 1836. ABC:1.3.1, vol. 2, p. 423.

14. Narcissa Prentiss to the secretaries of the ABCFM, 23 February 1835, ABCFM, "Correspondence."

15. O.S. Powell to the Secretaries of the ABCFM, 23 February 1835, ibid.

16. Marcus Whitman to David Greene, 3 March 1836, ibid.

17. Henry H. Spalding to the secretaries of the ABCFM, 7 August 1835, ibid. Spalding's personality quirks were attested to in a letter of recommendation written by Artemus Bullard; Bullard to Greene, 14 August 1835, ibid. Spalding himself confirmed this testimony in a letter to the board in which he admitted to a lack of discretion. Spalding to Greene, 2 March 1836, ibid.

18. Spalding to the secretaries of the ABCFM, 7 August 1835, ibid.

19. Whitman to Greene, 6 January 1836, ibid.

20. Whitman to Greene, 29 January 1836, ibid.

21. Whitman to Greene, 15 February 1836, ibid.

22. Spalding to Greene, 17 February 1836; and Whitman to 29 January 1836, ibid.

23. Whitman to Greene 3 March 1836, ibid.

24. Whitman to Greene, 3 March 1836; Greene to Whitman, 9 March 1836; and William Gray to the secretaries of the ABCFM, 17 February 1836, ibid.; Josephy, *Nez Perce Indians*, 146–147.

25. Whitman to Greene, 5 May 1836, ABCFM, "Correspondence."

26. Whitman to Greene, 5 May 1836, and Spalding to Greene, 8 July 1836, ibid.

27. Spalding to Greene, 8 July 1836, ibid.

28. Ibid.

29. Ibid.

30. Spalding to Greene, 20 September 1836, ABCFM, "Correspondence."

31. Ibid.

32. Whitman to Greene, 5 May 1837, in Theressa Gay, ed., "Spalding and Whitman Letters, 1837," 121.

33. Ibid.

34. Spalding to Greene, 16 February 1837, in Gay, "Spalding and Whitman Letters," 113–114.

35. Spalding to Greene, 20 September 1836, ABCFM, "Correspondence."

36. Whitman to Greene, 5 May 1837, in Gay, "Spalding and Whitman Letters," 124–125.

37. See ABCFM, "Correspondence."

38. For a full discussion of "received categories," see Marshall Sahlins, *Historical Metaphors and Mythical Realities*, 7.

39. Spalding to the secretaries of the ABCFM, 7 August 1835, ABCFM, "Correspondence."

40. Whitman to B. B. Wisner, 3 June 1834, and Narcissa Prentiss to the secretaries of the ABCFM, 23 February 1835, ibid.

41. Leon Festinger, Henry W. Reicken, and Stanley Schachter, *When Prophecy Fails*, 3.

42. Brown, "Missionaries and Cultural Diffusion," 214.

43. Phillips, *Protestant America*, 270–271.

44. Clifford M. Drury, ed., *The Diaries and Letters of Henry H. Spalding and Asa Bowen Smith Relating to the Nez Perce Mission*, 250n (hereafter cited as *Spalding and Smith Letters*); emphasis added. See also Berkhofer, *Salvation and the Savage*, 10.

45. Berkhofer, *Salvation and the Savage*, 70–72.

Chapter 7. The Converging Millennia

1. Asa Bowen Smith to Rufus Anderson, 25 October 1837, ABCFM, "Correspondence."

2. William Walker to David Greene, 15 October 1838, ibid.

3. Ibid.

4. Sisters of the Holy Names of Jesus and Mary, eds. *Gleanings of Fifty Years in the Northwest*, 35–41; Clarence B. Bagley, ed., *Early Catholic Missions in Old Oregon* 2:21, 76.

5. Henry Spalding to Mr. and Mrs. Bridges, 5 May 1840, in Henry Harmon Spalding, E. H. Spalding, and R. J. Spalding. Miscellaneous Reports, Documents, Papers, and Diaries of Eliza H. Spalding (1836–1840) and Henry Harmon Spalding (1836–1843) (hereafter cited as Spalding Papers).

6. Berkhofer, *Salvation and the Savage*, 156.

7. Henry Spalding to Mr. and Mrs. Bridges, 5 May 1840, Spalding Papers.

8. Smith to Greene, 3 September 1840, in Asa Bowen Smith, Letters to the American Board of Commissioners for Foreign Missions (hereafter cited as Smith Letters).

9. Ibid.

10. Pierre Jean de Smet, *Origin, Progress, and Prospects of the Catholic Mission to the Rocky Mountains*, 2–4.

11. Hiram M. Chittenden and A. T. Richardson, eds., *Life, Letters and Travels of Father Pierre-Jean De Smet, S.J.*, 39–40.

12. Sisters of the Holy Names, *Gleanings*, 46; Nicholas Point, "Recollections of the Rocky Mountains" 12:148; James W. Bashford, *The Oregon Missions*, 296; William N. Bischoff, *The Jesuits in Old Oregon*, 70; Bagley, *Early Catholic Missions* 2:51–52, 54.

13. Bagley, *Early Catholic Missions* 2:54; Bischoff, *Jesuits in Old Oregon*, 62–63.

14. Clifford M. Drury, ed., *First White Women over the Rockies*, 1:221.

15. Ibid. 1:221–222.

16. Henry Spalding to Greene, 12 February 1846, Spalding Papers.

17. Drury, *First White Women* 1:221.

18. J. M. Cataldo, "Sketch of the Nez Perce Indians" 9:44.

19. An excellent discussion of the Plan of Union and the doctrinal issues involved in both its formation and fragmentation may be found in Sydney E. Ahlstrom, *A Religious History of the American People*, 455–471. Though it stresses the personality issues overly, the best general treatment of the tensions in the Plateau mission may be found in Josephy, *Nez Perce Indians*, 194–200.

20. Drury, *Spalding and Smith Letters*, 145.

21. ABCFM, "Correspondence." See also Smith Letters; Drury, *Spalding and Smith Letters*; and Marcus Whitman and Narcissa Prentiss Whitman, Letters from Marcus Whitman, June 4, 1836–November 5, 1846 and from Narcissa Prentiss Whitman, March 15, 1836–October 12, 1847 (hereafter cited as Whitman Letters).

22. Allen, *Ten Years in Oregon*, 170.

23. Gay, "Spalding and Whitman Letters," 112.

24. Teaching by example was a key aspect of the entire approach of the ABCFM and was the primary excuse for the mission colony concept expressed in the Annual Report for 1827; Berkhofer, *Salvation and the Savage*, 89.

25. A full discussion of this issue would embroil the reader in the venerable and still unresolved "Did Whitman Save Oregon" controversy. The subject of a fifteen-year battle in the editorial pages of the Portland *Oregonian* (lasting from March 1885 until at least February 1900); a relatively famous exposition on historical criticism (Edward Gaylord Bourne, "The Legend of Marcus Whitman"); a spirited, if somewhat obscure, pamphlet defending Whitman's honor (by claiming that he was, indeed, an American imperialist) (Myron Eells, *A Reply to Professor Bourne's "The Whitman Legend"*); and untold pages in texts dealing with Oregon history, this battle ceased being of any major concern

long ago and was wisely ignored by Josephy in his *Nez Perce Indians*. The point of contention is whether or not Whitman returned to the United States during the winter of 1842 in order to warn the government that the British were maneuvering in preparation for seizing Oregon and if, in that effort, he caused the massive influx of settlers into the territory during the ensuing years. As Bourne points out, the primary materials do not support this interpretation, but Eells is also correct in asserting that the missionaries were concerned about the British (and Catholic) designs on the area. This was particularly true of William Gray, who reported his view in an 1870 book, *A History of Oregon*. As summarized by historian Robert J. Loewenberg: "Gray's *History* tells of a patriotic conspiracy under his leadership to win Oregon from a counter conspiracy of Jesuits and British monopolists"; Loewenberg, *Equality on the Oregon Frontier*. According to Gray, Whitman joined in this "patriotic conspiracy," and his ride to the States played a conspicuous role in the eventual victory; Gray, *History of Oregon*, 288–289. Undoubtedly concern about British and Catholic incursions, in conjunction with other forces, did influence the missionaries to encourage immigration as a means of protecting their missionizing efforts, but the imperialistic aspects should not be overemphasized.

26. Henry Spalding to Greene, 20 September 1836, ABCFM "Correspondence."

27. For the broad dissemination of news about Oregon, one need only peruse both the religious and secular periodicals of the time. According to Bourne, Horace Greeley "printed all the news relative to [Oregon] that he could gather." Elsewhere, Bourne gives negative evidence for Whitman's influence by stating that there is no record of Whitman's ride "in the *Globe* or the *National Intelligencer* among Washington papers, or in *Niles Register, although its pages for 1843 contain many insignificant items of Oregon News*" (emphasis added); Bourne, "Legend of Marcus Whitman," 85–86, 79–80.

28. Henry H. Spalding to Mrs. Hinsdale, 17 August 1842, Spalding Papers.

29. Drury, *First White Women* 1:158–159; 2:282, 249–250n.

30. Narcissa Whitman to Marcus Whitman, 4 October 1842, Whitman Letters.

31. Allen, *Ten Years in Oregon*, 177.

32. Ibid., 177, 181.

33. Henry Spalding to Mrs. Hinsdale, 17 August 1842, Spalding Papers.

34. Allen, *Ten Years in Oregon*, 185–190.

35. Ibid., 186–187.
36. Ibid., 190, 192.
37. This, again, involves the "Did Whitman Save Oregon" controversy. In this case, however, even Eells agrees that Whitman did not raise this party; Eells, *Reply to Professor Bourne*, 30. Instead it would appear that Whitman encountered the gathering mass in St. Louis while on his way back to Oregon and was pressed into service as a guide; see H. H. Bancroft, *History of Oregon* 2:390 and Bourne, "Legend of Marcus Whitman," 88–89.
38. Drury, *First White Women* 2:250n.
39. Allen, *Ten Years in Oregon*, 213–214.
40. Ibid., 214.
41. Ibid., 214–215.

Chapter 8. The World Will Fall to Pieces

1. Matilda J. [Sager] Delaney, *A Survivor's Recollections of the Whitman Massacre*, 11.
2. Allen, *Ten Years in Oregon*, 245–246.
3. Ibid., 246.
4. Ibid., 250; see also Drury, *First White Women* 2:288n, 305; A. Blanchet to G. Abernethy, 21 December 1847, in the *Oregon Spectator*, 20 January 1848.
5. Drury, *First White Women* 1:231.
6. Ibid. 1:143.
7. Delaney, *Survivor's Recollections*, 13.
8. Drury, *Spalding and Smith Letters*, 342.
9. A. Blanchet to Abernethy, 21 December 1847.
10. Delaney, *Survivor's Recollections*, 13; Drury, *Spalding and Smith Letters*, 342.
11. A. Blanchet to Abernethy, 21 December 1847.
12. Ibid.
13. Delaney, *Survivor's Recollections*, 13.
14. A. Blanchet to Abernethy, 21 December 1847; Delaney, *Survivor's Recollections*, 15.
15. Henry Spalding to A. Blanchet, 10 December 1847, in The *Oregon Spectator*, 20 January 1848.
16. Ibid.
17. A. Blanchet to Abernethy, 21 December 1847.
18. Bancroft, *History of Oregon* 1:693–694.

19. Josephy, *Nez Perce Indians*, 262–263; Drury, *Spalding and Smith Letters*, 343.

20. The best short account of this war is Josephy, *Nez Perce Indians*, 253–284, but one should not miss the classic account in Francis Fuller Victor, *Early Indian Wars of Oregon.*

21. *Oregon Spectator*, 13 July 1848.

22. Ibid.

23. Josephy, *Nez Perce Indians*, 292–293.

24. Andrew Jackson Splawn, *Ka-Mi-Akin*, 22.

25. Ibid.

26. Ibid., 23–24.

27. Ibid.

28. Ibid. The third was a Cayuse named Sticcus, who had befriended the Whitmans and had become their main confidant and informant.

29. Ibid.

30. Ibid.

31. James Doty, "A True Copy of the Record of the Official Proceedings at the Council in Walla Walla Valley, held jointly by Isaac I. Stevens & Joel Palmer on the Part of the U. States with the Tribes of Indians Named in the Treaties Made at that council, June 9 & 11, 1855," 11–28 (hereafter cited as Doty, "Record").

32. Ibid., 33–35.

33. Ibid., 35–37.

34. Ibid., 37–43.

35. Ibid., 43–44.

36. Ibid.

37. Ibid., 54.

38. Ibid.

39. Josephy, *Nez Perce Indians*, 327.

40. Doty, "Record," 79–86.

41. Josephy, *Nez Perce Indians*, 331.

42. Ibid.

43. Splawn, *Ka-Mi-Akin*, 35–36; Josephy, *Nez Perce Indians*, 336–337.

Epilogue

1. Maj. J. W. MacMurray, "The Dreamers of the Columbia River Valley in Washington Territory," 247; James Mooney, *The Ghost-Dance Religion*, 717.

2. MacMurray, "Dreamers of the Columbia," 247–248.

3. Mooney, *Ghost-Dance Religion*, 719.

4. Ibid.

5. Ibid.

6. Ibid., 724–725.

7. Ibid., 723.

8. MacMurray, "Dreamers of the Columbia," 247–248.

9. Mooney, *Ghost-Dance Religion*, 723.

10. Festinger, Riecken, and Schachter, *When Prophecy Fails*, 3.

11. Howard, *Nez Perce Joseph*, 15.

12. Spalding was so vehement in this belief that he had the statement "Jesuit missionaries were the leading cause of the Whitman Massacre" carved as an epitaph on his wife's tombstone; Drury, *First White Women* 1:232–233. He also became one of Oregon's leaders in the anti-Catholic, anti-immigrant political movement called the American party, more widely known as the Know-Nothings; see Malcolm Clark, Jr., "The Bigot Disclosed," 115–118.

13. Drury, *Spalding and Smith Letters*, 349. The most recent and authoritative work on the peace policy is Robert H. Keller, Jr., *American Protestantism and United States Indian Policy*.

14. The best general discussion of the relation between the "dreamer" faith and the outbreak of the Nez Perce War is in Josephy, *Nez Perce Indians*, 485–526; see also Howard, *Nez Perce Joseph*, iii, 47–49, 64.

15. In this regard, see Walker, *Conflict and Schism*.

Bibliography

Unpublished Sources

American Board of Commissioners for Foreign Missions. Papers of the American Board of Commissioners for Foreign Missions. Houghton Library, Harvard University. Cambridge, Mass.

—————. "Correspondence Relating to Applications of Missionaries to Oregon Territory, 1836–1839." Microfilm of Original Letters in the Houghton Library, Harvard University. Archives, San Francisco Theological Seminary, San Anselmo, Calif.

Doty, James. "A True Copy of the Record of the Official Proceedings at the Council in Walla Walla Valley, held jointly by Isaac I. Stevens & Joel Palmer on the Part of the U. States with the Tribes of Indians named in the Treaties made at that council, June 9 & 11, 1855." Manuscript Collection. Oregon Historical Society, Portland, Oreg.

Smith, Asa Bowen. Letters to the American Board of Commissioners for Foreign Missions, 1838–1840. Typescript of Original Letters in the Houghton Library, Harvard University. Manuscript Collection. Oregon Historical Society, Portland, Oreg.

Spalding, Henry Harmon, E. H. Spalding, and R. J. Spalding. Miscellaneous Reports, Documents, Papers, and Diaries of Eliza H. Spalding (1836–1840) and Henry Harmon Spalding (1836–1843). Manuscript Collection. Oregon Historical Society, Portland, Oreg.

Thompson, David. Journals, 1806–1812. Photocopies of Original Materials in the Public Archives, Ottowa, Canada. Manuscript Collection. Oregon Historical Society, Portland, Oreg.

Whitman, Marcus, and Narcissa P. Whitman. Letters from Marcus Whitman, 4 June 1836–5 November 1846; Letters from Narcissa Prentiss Whitman, 15 March 1836–12 October 1847. Microfilm of Original Letters in the Houghton Library, Harvard University. Manuscript Collection. Oregon Historical Society, Portland, Oreg.

Published Sources

Ahlstrom, Sydney E. *A Religious History of the American People*. New Haven, Conn.: Yale University Press, 1972.

Allen, A. J. *Ten Years in Oregon: Travels and Adventures of Doctor E. White and Lady, with incidents of two sea voyages via Sandwich Islands around Cape Horn, containing, also, a brief history of the missions. . . .* Ithaca, N.Y.: Andrus, Gauntlett, 1850.

Anastasio, Angelo. *Ethnohistory of the Spokan Indians*. Petitioners Exhibit 180, Indian Claims Commission Docket 47. Reprint. New York: Garland Press, 1974.

———. "The Southern Plateau: An Ecological Analysis of Intergroup Relations." *Northwest Anthropological Research Notes* 6 (1972): 109–229.

Angell, Robert C. *The Integration of American Society: A Study of Groups and Institutions*. New York: McGraw-Hill, 1941.

Antevs, Ernst. "Late Quaternary Climates in Arizona." *American Antiquity* 28 (1962): 193–98.

Aoki, Haruo. "Eastern Plateau Linguistic Diffusion Area." *International Journal of American Linguistics* 41 (1975): 183–199.

Attneave, Carolyn. "American Indians and Alaska Native Families: Emigrants in Their Own Homeland." In *Ethnicity and Family Therapy*, edited by Monica McGoldrick, John K. Pearce, and Joseph Giordano. New York: Guilford Press, 1982.

Axtell, James. *The European and the Indian: Essays in the Ethnohistory of Co-lonial North America*. New York: Oxford University Press, 1981.

Baerreis, David A. and Reid A. Bryson. "Climatic Episodes and the Dating of the Mississippian Culture." *Wisconsin Archaeologist* 46 (1965): 206–220.

Bagley, Clarence B., ed. *Early Catholic Missions in Old Oregon*. Seattle: Lowman and Hanford, 1932.

Bancroft, H. H. *History of Oregon*. 2 vols. San Francisco: The History Company, 1886–88.

Banner, Lois. "Religious Benevolence as Social Control: A Critique of American Interpretations." *Journal of American History* 60 (1973): 23–41.

Barnett, H. G. "Cultural Processes." *American Anthropologist* 42 (1940): 21–48.

Bashford, James W. *The Oregon Missions: The Story of How the Line Was Run between Canada and the United States*. New York: Abingdon, 1918.

Beal, Merrill. *"I Will Fight No More Forever": Chief Joseph and the Nez Perce War*. Seattle: University of Washington Press, 1971.

Beecher, Lyman. *A Plea for the West*. 2d ed. Cincinnati: Truman and Smith, 1835.

Benedict, Ruth F. *The Concept of the Guardian Spirit in North America*. Memoirs of the American Anthropological Association 29. Menasha, Wis.: American Anthropological Association, 1923.

Berkhofer, Robert F. *A Behavioral Approach to Historical Analysis*. New York: Free Press, 1969.

———. "Paradigms for Interpreting the Past: United States History." Paper presented at the annual meeting of the American Historical Association, December 29, 1983.

———. *Salvation and the Savage: An Analysis of Protestant Missions and American Indian Response, 1787–1862*. Lexington: University of Kentucky Press, 1965.

Billington, Ray Allen. "Anti-Catholic Propaganda and the Home Missionary Movement." *Mississippi Valley Historical Review* 21 (1935): 361–384.

———. *The Protestant Crusade, 1800–1860: A Study in the Origins of American Nativism*. New York: Macmillan, 1938.

Bischoff, William N. *The Jesuits in Old Oregon, 1840–1940*. Caldwell, Idaho: Caxton, 1945.

Boas, Franz, ed. *Folk-Tales of Salishan and Sahaptin Tribes*. Collected by

James A. Teit, Livingston Farrand, Marian K. Gould, and Herbert J. Spinden. Memoirs of the American Folklore Society 11. Lancaster, Pa.: American Folklore Society, 1917.

Bonner, T. D. *The Life and Adventures of James P. Beckworth, as Told to Thomas D. Bonner.* Edited by Delmont R. Oswald. Lincoln: University of Nebraska Press, 1972.

Bordon, Charles E. "Early Population Movements from Asia into Western North America." *Syesis* 2 (1969): 1–13.

———. "Notes and News: Great Basin and Plateau." *American Antiquity* 23 (1958): 453–454.

Bourne, Edward Gaylord. "The Legend of Marcus Whitman." In *Essays in Historical Criticism.* 1901. Reprint. Freeport, N.Y.: Books for Libraries, 1967.

Boyd, James Penny. *Recent Indian Wars, under the Lead of Sitting Bull and Other Chiefs: With a Full Account of the Messiah Craze, and Ghost Dances.* Philadelphia: Publishers Union, 1892.

Brackenridge, H. M. *Views of Louisiana.* 1814. Reprint. Chicago: Quadrangle, 1962.

Braudel, Fernand. *On History.* Translated by Sarah Matthews. Chicago: University of Chicago Press, 1980.

Brouillet, J. B. A. *Authentic Account of the Murder of Dr. Whitman and other Missionaries by the Cayuse Indians of Oregon in 1847.* 2d ed. Portland, Oreg., 1869.

Brown, G. Gordon. "Missionaries and Cultural Diffusion." *American Journal of Sociology* 50 (1944): 214–219.

Brunton, Bill B. "Ceremonial Integration in the Plateau of Northwestern America." *Northwest Anthropological Research Notes* 2 (1968): 1–28.

Bryson, Reid A., David A. Baerreis, and Wayne M. Wendland. "The Character of Late-glacial and Post-glacial Climatic Change." In *Pleistocene and Recent Environments of the Great Plains,* edited by Wakefield Dort, Jr. and J. Knox Jones, Jr. Lawrence: University of Kansas Press, 1970.

Burns, Robert I. *The Jesuits and the Indian Wars of the Northwest.* New Haven, Conn.: Yale University Press, 1966.

Burpee, L. J., ed. "York Fort to Blackfeet Country: The Journal of Anthony Hendry, 1754–1755." *Transactions of the Royal Society of Canada,* 1907, sec. 2: 307–360.

Butler, B. Robert. *A Guide to Understanding Idaho Archaeology.* 2d. rev. ed. Pocatello: Idaho Museum of Natural History, 1968.

————. *The Old Cordilleran Culture in the Pacific Northwest.* Occasional Papers of the Idaho State College Museum 5. Pocatello: Idaho Museum of Natural History, 1961.

Cataldo, J. M. "Sketch of the Nez Perce Indians." *Woodstock Letters* 9 (1880): 43–50, 109–118, 191–199; 10 (1881): 71–77, 198–204.

Chalfant, Stuart A. *Aboriginal Territory of the Nez Perce Indians.* Defendant's Exhibit 24, Indian Claims Commission Docket 175. Reprint. New York: Garland, 1974.

Chance, David H. *Influences of the Hudson's Bay Company on the Native Cultures of the Colvile District.* Memoirs of Northwest Anthropological Research Notes 2. Moscow, Idaho: Northwest Anthropological Research Notes, 1973.

Chittenden, Hiram M. *The American Fur Trade of the Far West.* Rev. ed. Stanford, Calif.: Academic Reprints, 1954.

Chittenden, Hiram M., and A. T. Richardson, eds. *Life, Letters and Travels of Father Pierre-Jean De Smet, S.J., 1801–1873.* 4 vols. New York: F. P. Harper, 1905.

Claiborne, Robert. *Climate, Man, and History.* New York: Norton, 1970.

Clark, Malcolm, Jr. "The Bigot Disclosed: 90 Years of Nativism." *Oregon Historical Quarterly* 75 (1974): 109–186.

Clements, Forrest E. *Primitive Concepts of Disease.* University of California Publications in American Archaeology and Ethnology 32. Berkeley and Los Angeles: University of California Press, 1932.

Coan, C. F. "The Adoption of the Reservation Policy in the Pacific Northwest, 1853–1855." *Oregon Historical Quarterly* 23 (1922): 1–38.

[Colton, Calvin], A Protestant. *Protestant Jesuitism.* New York: Harper and Brothers, 1836.

Commager, Henry Steele. *Jefferson, Nationalism, and the Enlightenment.* New York: Braziller, 1975.

Coues, Elliott, ed. *New Light on the Early History of the Greater Northwest: The Manuscript Journals of Alexander Henry, fur trader of the Northwest Company, and of David Thompson, official geographer and explorer of the same Company, 1799–1814; Exploration and adventure among the Indians on the Red, Saskatchewan, Missouri, and Columbia Rivers.* 3 vols. New York: F. P. Harper, 1897.

Cressman, Luther S. *Prehistory of the Far West: Homes of Vanished Peoples.* Salt Lake City: University of Utah Press, 1977.

Cronon, William. *Changes in the Land: Indians, Colonists, and the Ecology of New England.* New York: Hill and Wang, 1983.

Crosby, Alfred W. *The Columbian Exchange: Biological and Cultural Consequences of 1492.* Westport, Conn.: Greenwood, 1972.

Cross, Whitney R. *The Burned Over District: The Social and Intellectual History of Enthusiastic Religion in Western New York, 1800–1850.* Ithaca, N.Y.: Cornell University Press, 1950.

Dale, Harrison C., ed. *The Ashley-Smith Explorations and the Discovery of a Central Route to the Pacific, 1822–1829; with the original journals.* Cleveland: Arthur H. Clark Company, 1918.

Daugherty, Richard. *Early Man in the Columbia Intermontane Province.* Anthropological Papers of the University of Utah, Department of Anthropology 24. Salt Lake City: University of Utah Press, 1956.

———. "The Intermontain Western Tradition." *American Antiquity* 28 (1962): 144–150.

Davidson, Frederick Alexander. *The Effect of Floods on the Upstream Migration of the Salmon in the Columbia River.* Report to Public Utility District No. 2, Grant County, Oreg., March 1957.

Delaney, Matilda J. [Sager]. *A Survivor's Recollections of the Whitman Massacre.* Spokane, Wash.: Daughters of the American Revolution, 1920.

Dobyns, Henry F. "Estimating Aboriginal American Populations: An Appraisal of Techniques with a New Hemispheric Estimate." *Current Anthropology* 7 (1966): 395–416.

Douglas, David. *Journal Kept by David Douglas during His Travels in North America, 1823–1827.* London: W. Wesley, 1914.

Drury, Clifford M. *Chief Lawyer of the Nez Perces, 1796–1876.* Glendale, Calif.: Clark, 1979.

———. *Elkanah and Mary Walker: Pioneers among the Spokanes.* Caldwell, Idaho: Caxton, 1940.

———. *Henry Harmon Spalding.* Caldwell, Idaho: Caxton, 1936.

———. *Marcus and Narcissa Whitman and the Opening of Old Oregon.* Glendale, Calif.: Clark, 1970.

———. *Marcus Whitman, M.D.: Pioneer and Martyr.* Caldwell, Idaho: Caxton, 1937.

———. "The Nez Perce Delegation of 1831." *Oregon Historical Quarterly* 40 (1939): 283–287.

———. "Oregon Indians in the Red River School." *Pacific Historical Review* 7 (1938): 50–60.

———. "Protestant Missionaries in Oregon: A Bibliographic Survey." *Oregon Historical Quarterly* 50 (1949): 209–221.

————. ,ed. *The Diaries and Letters of Henry H. Spalding and Asa Bowen Smith Relating to the Nez Perce Mission, 1838–1842.* Glendale, Calif.: Clark, 1958.

————. ,ed. *First White Women over the Rockies: Diaries, Letters, and Biographical Sketches of Six Women of the Oregon Mission Who Made the Overland Journey in 1836 and 1838,* 3 vols. Glendale, Calif.: Clark, 1963, 1966.

————. ,ed. "The Spalding-Lowrie Correspondence." *Journal of the Department of History of the Presbyterian Church in the U.S.A.* 20 (1942): 1–114.

Dunn, John. *History of the Oregon Territory and the British American Fur Trade.* Philadephia: G. B. Zieber, 1845.

Durkheim, Emile. *Elementary Forms of Religious Life: A Study in Religious Sociology.* Translated by Joseph Ward Swain. Glencoe, Ill.: Free Press, 1926.

Dyen, Isidore. "Language Distribution and Migration Theory." *Language* 32 (1956): 611–626.

Eells, Myron. *A Reply to Professor Bourne's "The Whitman Legend."* Walla Walla, Wash.: Statesman Printing, 1902.

————. *Worship and Traditions of the Aborigines of America; or Their Testimony to the Religion of the Bible: Being a Paper read before the Victoria Institute, or Philosophical Society of Great Britain.* London: Victoria Institute, 1885.

Elliott, T. C., ed. "Journal of Alexander Ross." *Oregon Historical Quarterly* 14 (1913): 366–386.

Elmendorf, William. "Linguistic and Geographic Relations in the Northern Plateau Area." *Southwestern Journal of Anthropology* 21 (1965): 63–78.

Ewers, John C. *The Horse in Blackfoot Indian Culture, with Comparative Material from Other Western Tribes.* Bulletin of the Bureau of American Ethnology 159. Washington, D.C.: Government Printing Office, 1955.

Fahey, John. *The Flathead Indians.* Norman: University of Oklahoma Press, 1974.

Farrand, Livingston. "Notes on the Nez Perce Indians." *American Anthropologist* 33 (1921): 244–246.

Ferling, John. "The American Revolution and American Security: Whig and Loyalist Views." *Historian* 40 (1978): 492–507.

Ferris, Warren Angus. *Life in the Rocky Mountains: A Diary of Wanderings* on the Sources of the Rivers Missouri, Columbia, and Colorado from February, 1830 to November, 1855. Edited by Paul C. Phillips. Denver, Colo.: Old West, 1940.

Festinger, Leon, Henry W. Reicken, and Stanley Schachter. *When Prophecy Fails: A Social and Psychological Study of a Modern Group That Predicted the Destruction of the World*. 1956. Reprint. New York: Harper Torchbooks, 1964.

Franchere, Gabriel. *Franchere's Narrative of a Voyage to the Northwest Coast, 1810–1814*. Translated and edited by Hoyt C. Franchere. Norman: University of Oklahoma Press, 1967.

Fritts, Harold C., G. Robert Lofgren, and Geoffrey A. Gordon. "Past Climate Reconstruction from Tree Rings." *Journal of Interdisciplinary History* 10 (1980): 773–793.

Gabriel, Ralph H. "Evangelical Religion and Popular Romanticism in the Early Nineteenth Century." *Church History* 19 (1950): 34–47.

Gatke, Robert Moulton, ed. "A Document of Mission History, 1833–43." *Oregon Historical Quarterly* 36 (1935): 71–94, 163–171.

Gay, Theressa, ed. "Spalding and Whitman Letters, 1837." *Oregon Historical Quarterly* 37 (1936): 111-126.

Glover, Richard, ed. *David Thompson's Narrative, 1784–1812*. Publications of the Champlain Society 40. Toronto: Champlain Society, 1962.

Goodykoontz, Colin B. *Home Missions on the American Frontier, with Special Reference to the Home Missionary Society*. Caldwell, Idaho: Caxton, 1939.

Gray, William. *A History of Oregon, 1792–1849*. Portland, Oreg.: Harris and Holman, 1870.

Griffin, Clifford. *Their Brothers' Keepers: Moral Stewardship in the United States, 1800–1865*. New Brunswick, N.J.: Rutgers University Press, 1960.

Griffin, James B. "Some Correlations of Climatic and Cultural Change in Eastern North American Prehistory." *Annals of the New York Academy of Sciences* 95 (1961): 710–717.

Grinnell, George Bird. "Early Blackfoot History." *American Anthropologist* 2 (1892): 153–164.

Gunther, Erna. "The Westward Movement of Some Plains Traits." *American Anthropologist* 52 (1950): 174–180.

Haines, Francis. "The Nez Perce Delegation to St. Louis in 1831." *Pacific Historical Review* 6 (1937): 71–78.

————. "The Northward Spread of Horses among the Plains Indians." *American Anthropologist* 40 (1938): 429–437.

Hansen, Henry P. "Early Man in Oregon: Pollen Analysis and Postglacial Climate and Chronology." *Scientific Monthly* 62, supplement 7 (1946): 52–62.

————. "Postglacial Forest Seccession, Climate, and Chronology in the Pacific Northwest." *Transactions of the American Philosophical Society*, n.s. 37 (1947): pt. 1.

Henry, Alexander. *Travels and Adventures in Canada and the Indian Territories between the Years 1760 and 1776.* New York: I. Riley, 1809.

Highwater, Jamake. *The Primal Mind: Vision and Reality in Indian America.* New York: Harper and Row, 1981.

Horsman, Reginald. *Race and Manifest Destiny: The Origin of American Racial Anglo-Saxonism.* Cambridge, Mass.: Harvard University Press, 1981.

Howard, Oliver Otis. *Nez Perce Joseph: An Account of His Ancestors, His Lands, His Confederates, His Enemies, His Murders, His War, His Pursuit and Capture.* Boston, Mass.: Lee and Shepard, 1881.

Hulbert, Archer B., ed. *The Charles B. Voorhis Series of Overland to the Pacific: A Narrative-Documentary History of the Great Epics of the Far West.* 8 vols. Colorado Springs: The Stewart Commission of Colorado College and the Denver Public Library, 1933–1938.

Huntington, Ellsworth. *The Climatic Factor as Illustrated in Arid America.* Publications of the Carnegie Institution of Washington 192. Washington, D.C.: Carnegie Institution, 1914.

Hyde, George. *Indians of the High Plains: From the Prehistoric Period to the Coming of the Europeans.* Norman: University of Oklahoma Press, 1959.

Jacobs, Wilbur R. *Dispossessing the American Indian: Indians and Whites on the Colonial Frontier.* New York: Scribner's, 1972.

Jefferson, Thomas. *Notes on the State of Virginia.* Edited by William Peden. 1955. Reprint. New York: Norton, 1972.

————. *The Writings of Thomas Jefferson.* Edited by Albert Ellery Bergh. 20 vols. Washington, D.C.: Thomas Jefferson Memorial Association, 1904–1905.

Josephy, Alvin M. *The Nez Perce Indians and the Opening of the Northwest.* New Haven, Conn.: Yale University Press, 1965.

Keller, Robert H., Jr. *American Protestantism and United States Indian Policy, 1869–1882.* Lincoln: University of Nebraska Press, 1983.

Kelley, Hall Jackson. "To a Member of Congress, on the Settlement of the Oregon Country, No. 1." *American Traveller* 8, no. 6 (1832): 1.

———. "To a Member of Congress, on the Settlement of the Oregon Country, No. 8." *American Traveller* 8, no. 20 (1832): 1.

———. "To a Member of Congress, on the Settlement of the Oregon Country, No. 9." *American Traveller* 8, no. 21 (1832): 1.

Kip, Lawrence. *The Indian Council of Walla Walla*. Sources of the History of Oregon 1. Eugene, Oreg.: Star Job Office, 1897.

Kroeber, A. L. "Stimulus Diffusion." *American Anthropologist* 42 (1940): 1–20.

Lamb, H. H. *Climate: Present, Past, and Future*. 2 vols. London: Methuen, 1972.

Lamb, Sydney M. "Linguistic Prehistory in the Great Basin." *International Journal of American Linguistics* 24 (1958): 95–100.

Lee, Daniel, and J. H. Frost. *Ten Years in Oregon*. New York: J. Collord, Printer for the authors, 1844.

Lee, Jason. "The Diary of Jason Lee." *Oregon Historical Quarterly* 17 (1916): 116–146, 240–266, 397–430.

Leonard, Ira M., and Robert D. Parmet. *American Nativism, 1830–1860*. New York: Van Nostrand Reinhold, 1971.

Leonhardy, Frank C., and David G. Rice. "A Proposed Culture Typology for the Lower Snake River Region, Southeastern Washington." *Northwest Anthropological Research Notes* 4 (1970): 1–29.

Le Roy Ladurie, Emmanuel, *Times of Feast, Times of Famine: A History of Climate since the Year 1000*. Translated by Barbara Bray. Garden City, N.Y.: Doubleday, 1971.

Levi-Strauss, Claude. *The Savage Mind*. Chicago: University of Chicago Press, 1966.

Lewis, Oscar. *Effects of White Contact upon Blackfoot Culture with Special Reference to the Role of the Fur Trade*. Monographs of the American Ethnological Society 6. 1941. Reprint. Seattle: University of Washington Press, 1966.

Lewis, William S. "The Case of Spokane Garry." *Bulletin of the Spokane Historical Society* 1 (1917): 2–68.

Linton, Ralph. "Nativistic Movements." *American Anthropologist* 45 (1943): 230–240.

Loewenberg, Robert J. *Equality on the Oregon Frontier: Jason Lee and the Methodist Mission, 1834–1843*. Seattle: University of Washington Press, 1976.

Luria, A. R. *Cognitive Development: Its Cultural and Social Foundations*.

Translated by Martin Lopez-Morillas and Lynn Solotaroff. Edited by Michael Cole. Cambridge, Mass.

McBeth, Kate. *Nez Perces since Lewis and Clark*. New York: Revell, 1908.

McDermott, L. "Folk-lore of the Flathead Indians of Idaho." *Journal of American Folklore* 14 (1901): 240–251.

Mackenzie, Charles. "The Missouri Indians: A Narrative of Four Trading Expeditions to the Missouri, 1804, 1805, 1806 for the North-West Company." In *Les bourgeois de la Compagnie du Nord-Ouest*, edited by Louis Masson. Quebec: A. Cote, 1889–1890.

McLeod, Alexander. *A Scriptural View of the Character, Causes, and Ends of the Present War*. New York: Eastburn, Kirk; Whiting and Watson; and Smith and Forman, 1815.

MacMurray, Maj. J. W. "The Dreamers of the Columbia River Valley in Washington Territory." *Transactions of the Albany Institute* 11 (1887):240–248.

McNeill, William, *Plagues and Peoples*. New York: Doubleday, Anchor, 1976.

McWhorter, Lucellus V. *Hear Me, My Chiefs! Nez Perce History and Legend*. Caldwell, Idaho: Caxton, 1952.

———. *Yellow Wolf: His Own Story*. Caldwell, Idaho: Caxton, 1940.

Madsen, Brigham D. *The Bannock of Idaho*. Caldwell, Idaho: Caxton, 1958.

———. *The Lemhi: Sacajawea's People*. Caldwell, Idaho: Caxton, 1980.

Malouf, Carling, and A. Arline Malouf. "The Effects of Spanish Slavery on the Indians of the Intermountain West." In *The Emergent Native Americans: A Reader in Culture Contact*, edited by Deward E. Walker, Jr. Boston: Little, Brown, 1971.

Marsden, George M. *The Evangelical Mind and the New School Presbyterian Experience: A Case Study of Thought and Theology in Nineteenth-Century America*. New Haven, Conn.: Yale University Press, 1970.

Martin, Calvin. "Ethnohistory: A Better Way to Write Indian History." *Western Historical Quarterly* 9 (1978): 41–56.

———. *Keepers of the Game: Indian-Animal Relationships and the Fur Trade*. Berkeley and Los Angeles: University of California Press, 1978.

Masson, Louis R., ed. *Les bourgeois de la Compagnie du Nord-Ouest*. 2 vols. Quebec: A. Cote, 1889–1890.

Mathews, Donald C. "The Second Great Awakening as an Organizing Process: An Hypothesis." *American Quarterly* 25 (1969): 23–43.

Mead, Sidney E. *The Lively Experiment: The Shaping of Christianity in America*. New York: Harper and Row, 1963.

Merk, Frederick. *Manifest Destiny and Mission in American History: A Reinterpretation.* New York: Knopf, 1963.

————., ed. *Fur Trade and Empire: George Simpson's Journal.* Cambridge, Mass.: Belknap, of Harvard University Press, 1968.

Miller, Perry. *The Life of the Mind in America: From Revolution to the Civil War.* New York: Harcourt, Brace and World, 1965.

Mishkin, Bernard. *Rank and Warfare among the Plains Indians.* Monographs of the American Ethnological Society 3. Locust Valley, N.Y.: American Ethnological Society, 1940.

Miyakawa, T. Scott. *Protestants and Pioneers: Individualism and Conformity on the American Frontier.* Chicago: University of Chicago Press, 1964.

Mooney, James. *The Ghost-Dance Religion.* Annual Report of the Bureau of American Ethnology 14. Washington, D.C.: Government Printing Office, 1896.

Morse, Samuel F. B. *The Foreign Conspiracy against the Liberties of the United States. The numbers of Brutus, originally published in the New-York Observer.* New York: Leavitt, Lord, 1835.

————. *Imminent Dangers to the Free Institutions of the United States through Foreign Immigration and the Present State of the Naturalization Laws. A series of numbers originally published in the New-York Journal of Commerce.* New York: E. B. Clayton, 1835.

Morton, Arthur S., ed. *The Journal of Duncan M'Gillivray of the Northwest Company at Fort George on the Saskatchewan, 1794–1795.* Toronto: Macmillan, 1929.

Murphy, Robert F., and Yolanda Murphy. *Shoshone-Bannock Subsistence and Society.* Anthropological Records of the University of California 16. Berkeley and Los Angeles: University of California Press, 1960.

Nasatir, Abraham Phineas, ed. *Before Lewis and Clark: Documents Illustrating the History of the Missouri, 1785–1804.* St. Louis, Mo.: St. Louis Historical Documents Foundation, 1952.

Norbeck, Edward. *Religion in Primitive Society.* New York: Harper, 1961.

North, Douglass C. *The Economic Growth of the United States, 1790–1860.* Rev. ed. New York: Norton, 1966.

Oglesby, Richard E. *Manuel Lisa and the Opening of the Missouri Fur Trade.* Norman: University of Oklahoma Press, 1963.

Oliphant, J. Orin. "George Simpson and the Oregon Missions." *Pacific Historical Review* 6 (1937): 213–248.

————., ed. "Documents Illustrating the Presbyterian Advance into the Oregon Country." *Washington Historical Quarterly* 26 (1935): 123–128, 202–224, 280–301.

Packard, R. L. "Notes on the Mythology and Religion of the Nez Perce." *Journal of American Folklore* 4 (1891): 327–330.

Palladino, Lawrence B. *Indian and White in the Northwest: A History of Catholicity in Montana, 1831–1891.* 2d. ed. Lancaster, Pa.: Wickersham, 1922.

Parker, Rev. Samuel. *Journal of an Exploring Tour Beyond the Rocky Mountains; Under the Direction of the A.B.C.F.M., performed in the years 1835, '36, and '37.* Ithaca, N.Y.: Published for the author by Mack, Andrus, and Woodruff, 1838.

Pessen, Edward. "The Egalitarian Myth and the American Social Reality: Wealth, Mobility, and Equality in the 'Era of the Common Man.'" *American Historical Review* 76 (1971): 989–1034.

Phillips, Clifton Jackson. *Protestant America and the Pagan World: The First Half Century of the American Board of Commissioners for Foreign Missions, 1810–1860.* Cambridge, Mass.: East Asian Research Center, Harvard University, 1968.

Point, Nicholas. "Recollections of the Rocky Mountains." *Woodstock Letters* 11 (1882): 298–321; 12 (1883): 3–22; 13 (1884): 3–13.

Powell, Fred W. "Hall Jackson Kelly, Prophet of Oregon." *Oregon Historical Quarterly* 18 (1917): 93–139, 167–224, 271–295.

————., ed. *Hall Jackson Kelley on Oregon: A Collection of Five of His Published Works and a Number of Hitherto Unpublished Letters.* Princeton, N.J.: Princeton University Press, 1932.

Rabb, Theodore K. *The Struggle for Stability in Early Modern Europe.* New York: Oxford University Press, 1975.

Ranulf, Svend. *Moral Indignation and Middle Class Psychology: A Sociological Study.* 1938. Reprint. New York: Schocken, 1964.

Ray, Verne F. "The Columbia Indian Confederacy: A League of Central Plateau Tribes." In *Culture in History; Essays in Honor of Paul Radin.* edited by Stanley Diamond. New York: Columbia University Press for Brandeis University, 1960.

————. *Cultural Relations in the Plateau of Northwestern America.* Los Angeles: The Southwestern Museum, 1939.

————. *Ethnohistory of the Joseph Band of Nez Perce Indians, 1805–1905.* Petitioner's Exhibit 75, Indian Claims Commission Docket 186. Reprint. New York: Garland, 1974.

————. *The Sanpoil and Nespelem: Salishan Peoples of Northeastern Washington*. University of Washington Publications in Anthropology 5. Seattle: University of Washington Press, 1933.

Redfield, Robert, Ralph Linton, and Melville J. Herskovits (Social Science Research Council Committee on Acculturation). "Memorandum for the Study of Acculturation." *American Anthropologist* 38 (1936): 149–152.

Reeves, Brian. "On the Coalescence of the Laurentide and Cordilleran Ice Sheets in the Western Interior of North America with Particular Reference to the Southern Alberta Area." In *Aboriginal Man and Environments on the Plateau of Northwest America*. edited by Arnoud Stryd and Rachel Smith. Calgary: Students' Press, 1971.

Rich, E. E. *The Fur Trade and the Northwest to 1857*. Canadian Centenary Series 2. Toronto: McClelland and Stewart, 1967.

————. *The History of the Hudson's Bay Company, 1670–1870*. 3 vols. New York: Macmillan, 1961.

————., ed. *Cumberland House Journals and Inland Journal, 1775–82*. 2 vols. Publications of the Hudson's Bay Record Society 14–15. London: Hudson's Bay Record Society, 1951–1952.

Ross, Alexander. *Fur Hunters of the Far West: A Narrative of Adventures in the Oregon and Rocky Mountains*. Edited by Milo M. Quaife. 2d ed. Chicago: Donnelley, 1924.

Sahlins, Marshall. *Historical Metaphors and Mythical Realities: Structure in the Early History of the Sandwich Islands Kingdom*. Ann Arbor: University of Michigan Press, 1981.

Sandeen, Ernest R. *The Roots of Fundamentalism: British and American Millenarianism, 1800–1930*. Chicago: University of Chicago Press, 1970.

Sanger, David "Cultural Traditions in the Interior of British Columbia." *Syesis* 2 (1969): 189–200.

————. "Prehistory of the Pacific Northwest Plateau as Seen From the Interior of British Columbia." *American Antiquity* 32 (1967): 186–197.

Secoy, Frank R. *Changing Military Patterns on the Great Plains: Seventeenth Century Through Early Nineteenth Century*. Monographs of the American Ethnological Society 21. Locust Valley, N.Y.: American Ethnological Society, 1953.

Sheehan, Bernard. *Seeds of Extinction: Jeffersonian Philanthropy and the American Indian*. Chapel Hill: University of North Carolina Press, 1973.

Shimkin, Dimitri Boris. "Shoshoni-Commanche Origins and Migrations." *Proceedings of the Sixth Pacific Science Congress* (1941) 4: 17–25.

Sisters of the Holy Names of Jesus and Mary, eds. *Gleanings of Fifty Years in the Northwest, 1859–1909.* Portland, Oreg.: Glass and Prudhomme, 1909.

Slickpoo, Allen P. *Noon nee-me-poo (We, the Nez Perce): Culture and History of the Nez Perces.* Lapwai, Idaho: Nez Perce Tribal Council, 1973.

———. *Nu Mee poom tit wah tit (Nez Perce Legends).* Lapwai, Idaho: Nez Perce Tribal Council, 1972.

Smet, Pierre Jean, de. *Origin, Progress and Prospects of the Catholic Mission to the Rocky Mountains.* Philadelphia: Fithian, 1843.

Smith, James Ward, and A. L. Jamison, *Religious Perspectives in American Culture.* Princeton, N.J.: Princeton University Press, 1961.

———. *The Shaping of American Religion.* Princeton, N.J.: Princeton University Press, 1961.

Smith, Marian W. "The War Complex of the Plains Indians." *Proceedings of the American Philosophical Society* 78 (1938): 425–464.

Smith, Timothy L. *Revivalism and Social Reform in Mid-nineteenth Century America.* New York: Abingdon, 1957.

Spier, Leslie. *The Prophet Dance of the Northwest and Its Derivatives.* American Anthropological Association, General Series in Anthropology 1. Menasha, Wis.: American Anthropological Association, 1935.

———, ed. *The Sinkaietk or Southern Okanagon of Washington.* American Anthropological Association, General Series in Anthropology 6. Menasha, Wis.: American Anthropological Association, 1938.

Spinden, Herbert J. *The Nez Perce Indians.* Memoirs of the American Anthropological Association 9. Menasha, Wis.: American Anthropological Association, 1908.

———. "Nez Perce Tales." *Journal of American Folklore* 21 (1908): 149–158.

Splawn, Andrew Jackson. *Ka-Mi-Akin: Last Hero of the Yakimas.* Portland, Oreg.: Binsford and Mort for the Oregon Historical Society, 1917.

Stevens, Isaac I. "Narrative and Final Report of Explorations for a Route for a Pacific Railroad, near the forty-seventh and forty-ninth parallels of North latitude." In U. S. War Department, *Reports of Explorations and Surveys, to ascertain the most practical and economical Route for a Railroad from the Mississippi River to the Pacific*

Ocean, vol. 12. Washington, D.C.: Government Printing Office, 1860.

———. *Pacific Railroad—Northern Route; Letter to the Railroad Convention of Washington and Oregon called to meet at Vancouver, W.T., May 20, 1860*. Portland, Oreg., 1860.

Steward, Julian. *Basin-Plateau Aboriginal Sociopolitical Groups*. Bulletin of the Bureau of American Ethnology 120. Washington, D.C.: Government Printing Office, 1938.

Stryd, Arnoud, and Rachel Smith, eds. *Aboriginal Man and Environments on the Plateau of Northwest America*. Calgary: Students' Press, 1971.

Suttles, Wayne. "Coping With Abundance; Subsistence on the Northwest Coast." In *Man the Hunter*, edited by Richard B. Lee and Irven DeVore. Chicago: Aldine, 1968.

———. "The Plateau Prophet Dance among the Coast Salish." *Southwestern Journal of Archaeology* 13 (1957): 352–396.

Swadesh, Morris. "The Linguistic Approach to Salish Prehistory." In *Indians of the Urban Northwest*, edited by Marion W. Smith. Columbia University Contributions to Anthropology 36. New York: Columbia University Press, 1949.

Swanson, Earl H., Jr. "Approach to Culture History in the Pacific Northwest." *Southwestern Journal of Anthropology* 17 (1961): 140–145.

———. "Early Cultures in Northwestern America." *American Antiquity* 28 (1962): 151–158.

———. *The Emergence of Plateau Culture*. Occasional Papers of the Idaho State College Museum 8. Pocatello: Idaho Museum of Natural History, 1962.

Sweet, William W. *American Culture and Religion: Six Essays*. Dallas, Tex.: Southern Methodist University Press, 1951.

———. *Religion in the Development of American Culture, 1765–1840*. New York: Scribner's, 1952.

———. *Revivalism in America: Its Origin, Growth, and Decline*. New York: Scribner's, 1944.

Taylor, George Rogers. *The Transportation Revolution, 1815–1860*. New York: Harper and Row, 1968.

Taylor, H. C., and L. L. Hoaglin, Jr. "The 'Intermittent Fever' Epidemic of the 1830's on the Lower Columbia River." *Ethnohistory* 9 (1978): 160–178.

Teit, James A. *The Salishan Tribes of the Western Plateaus*. Annual Report of the Bureau of American Ethnology 45. Washington, D.C.: Government Printing Office, 1930.

Thomas, Keith. *Religion and the Decline of Magic*. New York: Scribner's, 1971.

Thwaites, Reuben Gold, ed. *The Jesuit Relations and Allied Documents: Travels and Explorations of the Jesuit Missionaries in New France, 1610– 1791*. 73 vols. Cleveland: Burrows, 1899.

————., ed. *Original Journals of the Lewis and Clark Expedition, 1804– 1806*. 8 vols. New York: Dodd, Mead, 1904–1905.

Turney-High, Harry H. *Ethnography of the Kutenai*. Memoirs of the American Anthropological Association 56. Menasha, Wis.: American Anthropological Association, 1941.

————. *The Flathead Indians of Montana*. Memoirs of the American Anthropological Association 48. Menasha, Wis.: American Anthropological Association, 1937.

Tuveson, Ernest Lee. *Redeemer Nation: The Idea of America's Millennial Role*. Chicago: University of Chicago Press, 1968.

U. S. Congress. *Abridgement of Debates in Congress from 1789 to 1856*. 16 vols. Edited by Thomas Hart Benton. New York: Appleton, 1857–1861.

————. *American State Papers: Indian Affairs, Documents, Legislative and Executive of the Congress of the United States, from the First Session of the First to the Second Session of the Nineteenth Congress inclusive; Commencing March 3, 1789 and ending March 3, 1827*. 2 vols. Washington, D.C.: Gales and Seaton, 1832–1834.

————. *American State Papers: Military Affairs, Documents, Legislative and Executive of the Congress of the United States, from the First Session of the First to the Second Session of the Twenty-fifth Congress inclusive; Commencing March 3, 1789 and ending March 3, 1838*. 7 vols. Washington, D.C.: Gales and Seaton, 1836–1861.

————. *Annals of Congress*.

————. *Register of Debates in Congress*.

U. S. Department of the Census. *Historical Statistics of the United States: Colonial Times to 1970*. Washington, D.C.: Government Printing Office, 1975.

Van Deusen, Glyndon G. *The Jacksonian Era, 1828–1848*. New York: Harper and Row, 1959.

Victor, Francis Fuller. *Early Indian Wars of Oregon*. Salem, Oreg.: F. C. Baker, 1894.

Voegelin, Carl F., and Florence M. Voegelin. "Languages of the World: Native American Fascicle One." *Anthropological Linguistics* 6 (1964): 1–149.

———. "Languages of the World: Native American Fascicle Two." *Anthropological Linguistics* 7 (1965): pt. 1.

———. *Map of North American Indian Languages*. Publications of the American Ethnological Society 20. Rev. ed. New York: American Ethnological Society, 1966.

Walker, Deward E., Jr. *American Indians of Idaho*. Vol. 1, *Aboriginal Cultures*. Anthropological Monographs of the University of Idaho 2. Moscow: University of Idaho Press, 1973.

———. *Conflict and Schism in Nez Perce Acculturation: A Study of Religion and Politics*. Pullman: Washington State University Press, 1968.

———. *Mutual Crossutilization of Economic Resources in the Plateau: An Example from Aboriginal Nez Perce Fishing Practices*. Washington State University Laboratory of Anthropology, Report of Investigations 41. Pullman: Washington State University Press, 1967.

———. "New Light on the Prophet Dance Controversy." *Ethnohistory* 3 (1969): 245–255.

———. "A Nez Perce Ethnographic Observation of Archaeological Significance." *American Antiquity* 31 (1966): 436–437.

Wallace, Anthony F. C. *The Death and Rebirth of the Seneca*. New York: Knopf, 1969.

———. "Revitalization Movements." *American Anthropologist* 58 (1956): 264–281.

Washburn, Wilcomb E. "Symbol, Utility, and Aesthetics in the Indian Fur Trade." In *Aspects of the Fur Trade: Selected Papers of the 1965 North American Fur Trade Conference*, edited by Dale L. Morgan. St. Paul, Minn.: Minnesota Historical Society, 1968.

Webb, Thompson, III. "The Reconstruction of Climatic Sequences from Botanical Data." *Journal of Interdisciplinary History* 10 (1980): 749–772.

Wedel, Waldo. "Culture Sequence in the Central Great Plains." *Smithsonian Miscellaneous Collections* 100 (1940): 291–352.

———. "Environment and Native Subsistence Economies in the Central Great Plains." *Smithsonian Miscellaneous Collections* 101 (1941): No. 3.

Weinberg, Albert K. *Manifest Destiny: A Study of Nationalist Expansionism in American History*. Baltimore: Johns Hopkins Press, 1935.

Wentzel, W. F. "Letters to the Hon. Roderick McKenzie, 1807–1824."

In *Les bourgeois de la Compagnie du Nord-Ouest*, edited by Louis R. Masson. Quebec: A. Cote, 1889–1890.

Whalen, Sue. "The Nez Perces' Relationship to Their Land." *The Indian Historian* 4, no. 3 (1971): 30–33.

Whitman, Marcus. "Journal and Report by Dr. Marcus Whitman of His Tour of Exploration with Rev. Samuel Parker in 1825 Beyond the Rocky Mountains." Edited by F. S. Young. *Oregon Historical Quarterly* 28 (1927): 239–257.

Whorf, Benjamin L. "An American Indian Model of the Universe." In *Language, Thought, and Reality: The Selected Writings of Benjamin Lee Whorf*, edited by John B. Carroll. Cambridge, Mass.: Technology Press of the Massachusetts Institute of Technology, 1956.

Wilkes, Charles. *Narrative of the United States Exploring Expedition during the years 1838, 1839, 1840, 1841, and 1842*. 5 vols. Philadelphia: Lea and Blanchard, 1845.

Williams, Glyndwr, ed. *Peter Skene Ogden's Snake Country Journals, 1827–28 and 1828–29*. Publications of the Hudson's Bay Record Society 28. London: Hudson's Bay Record Society, 1971.

Williamson, Chilton. *American Suffrage from Property to Democracy, 1760–1860*. Princeton, N.J.: Princeton University Press, 1960.

Index

Abernethy, George, 107–108, 110

Adams, S., 72

Ahlstrom, Sydney E., 142 n.19

American Board of Commissioners for Foreign Missions (ABCFM): conflict within Protestant movement and, 95–96, 98; Manifest Destiny and, 73; response to Flathead delegation by, 78, 79–86

American Traveller, 74

Animals: killing of, 15; slaughter of Indian dogs, 91–92

Aristocracy: horse-derived status and Indian, 39–40; political theory and early American, 65

Arminian theology, 89

Ashley, William, 58

Bancroft, H. H., 108

Banner, Lois, 138 n.38

Beal, Merrill, 5

Beecher, Lyman, 69, 80, 94

Benton, Thomas Hart, 68, 72

Berkhofer, Robert, 2, 91

Bible, 70. *See also* Book mentioned by Indian Prophets

Bischoff, William Norbert, 93

Black Robes. *See* Catholic missionaries

Blanchet, Francis Norbert, 90, 92, 107–108

Boas, Franz, 5

Book mentioned by Indian Prophets, 45, 52, 61. *See also* Bible

Bourne, Edward Gaylord, 142 n.25, 143 n.27, 144 n.37

167